LOVED BACK TO LIFE SERIES

CITY OF HOPE
An Autobiography of Love
By Pearl Sunshine

SCP – Shepherds Care Publishing

© SCPublishing / Shepherds Care Counseling Ministries
2473 S. Higley Road - Suite 104 PMB 210
Gilbert, Arizona 85295

Loved Back to Life Series

City of Hope

An Autobiography of Love

By Pearl Sunshine

Editorial Supervision: Michael E. Chalberg
Paperback Edition – ISBN 978-0-9746464-6-4 Revised
Ebook Edition – 978-1-7349703-8-8

Order: scpublishing@shepherdscareministries.org
Email: Pearl.Sunshine@scpublishing.org
Web: www.shepherdscareministries.org
Editor: scpublishing2020@gmail.com

TABLE OF CONTENTS

"Blessed are the pure in heart,
For they shall see God."

I

Forward by SCPublishing

Our new collections of autobiographies entitled: **_Loved Back to Life Series_,** are being presented to all who have lost hope in the power of God's unconditional love...to heal and redeem His purposes for our lives. We live in both the physical realm and the larger spiritual realm simultaneously, yet it is the physical experience which often defines our understanding of spiritual realities. So, we seek to find meaning to these realities, when we encounter suffering and pain, rejection and condemnation in our relationships with others...who are supposed to love, nurture, provide for our needs and teach us the truth about why our Heavenly Father created us to have an eternal relationship with Him.

When this relationship is broken by evil's influence, through control of those around and over us...we lose hope and trust in the power of God's love to overcome this evil and we cry out to the Lord, *"You would have been kinder to never have created me...just let me die."* This is often our primary mistake in seeking answers to why it seems that God isn't answering our prayers and we feel abandoned by Him as though our condition means we are unworthy of His love and presence in our lives. We are afraid to trust in and hope for, the fulfillment of God's promises and purpose for us in Christ Jesus. This is why this first autobiographical set by Pearl Sunshine is given in her own words, changing only names of those involved, without holding back any reality of abuses by evil controlling her life. The drawings given of the actual events from early childhood, depicting clearly the actions of others... family and Satanic cults can be triggering of painful memories for readers who are themselves survivors of such abuses. We ask that the readers have the strength and courage to continue reading when possible, to discover the joys as well of being drawn into God's heart. Her purpose here is not to convince anyone of the truth of evil in our lives, or her strength in continuing to follow the path that Jesus has set for her, to trust God's love again.

Her purpose, and ours, is to challenge our readers to understand more fully why Jesus is calling to us to trust in Him, and His love to heal and redeem us to do for us what we can't do for ourselves...without Him. If we can believe in the promises that; **"I will never leave nor forsake you"**, **"I will come to you in the darkest depths and overcome the evil to set you free"**, **"I will love you back to life... eternal life with me"** and **"In this world you will have tribulations, but rejoice for I have overcome this world,"** then we can know the truth of who Jesus is in this life, and trust again in the plans and purposes of our Father God's unconditional love in action... right now... right here, where you are at. If these autobiographies, and the ones to follow in this series, help you to seek a renewed relationship of trust in Him...then the suffering you read about followed by their free will choices to continue on the journey, will have been worth it to each author. The introduction of Pearl by Jesus can challenge us all about what He means by saying, **"My grace is sufficient for you, for my power is made perfect in weakness."** This is the power of God's love freely given to us to survive this world with Him until we go home.

Ultimately these books and the others that will follow in this series, are about the personal commitment that God makes to each one of us to bring healing, as revealed in these private journals of one group of people with Dissociative Identity Disorder (DID) or Multiple Personality Disorder (MPD), who accepted God's call to receive His promise of healing for 'wholeness' in Him... living as one person with Him.

Our first series of books, *Shattered People: Journeys to Joy - Love,* focused on specific issues of people with DID and their struggle to receive healing later in life so they could be 'acceptable' to be loved by family and relationships in their closest circumstances. I offer commentary and counseling in this series as pastor, friend and counselor for them to promote treatment methods and dialogue about trauma and abuse survival, especially about our common questions to God on suffering, survival and how we all can know God through relationships within community and in our one on one time with Him. .

This series however, *Loved Back to Life,* looks at the individual searching for meaning and purpose directly from God in conversation with Him, expecting answers from no one else... not counseling or outside help for most of their lives. They seek meaning for a lifetime of feeling alone in darkness... evil that defined who they were, before discovering they were never alone

How they and Pearl come to trust in Jesus' love placed very deep in their soul long ago was as hard to believe for them, as the memories of suffering being revealed as true by those who had endured them... and the healing Jesus gives to both. These books allow you the reader to learn from their struggle to know God... to trust Jesus... to accept the Holy Spirit and their will for her life and how receiving God's love is the purpose of her life... a purpose she now wishes to share with all who suffer... to risk allowing Jesus in with His answers for healing.

Editor & Fellow Servant – Pastor Mike

Review:

Dr. Joe Johnson, pastoral counselor. D.Min.
Fuller Seminary 4/2020

"Pearl's miraculous story of redemption, healing, recovery and freedom from unspeakable suffering is a witness to what most people would say is impossible when they read these books. God brings Pastor Mike alongside of Pearl to share his love of Jesus to witness in confidence the power of Jesus to redeem and minister healing to Pearl, including each one of her dissociative parts (*alters*) more than I have ever known. Pearl opens her heart wide to the readers to the many ways she is healing and recovering from incredible abuses physically, emotionally and spiritually. I have learned that the biggest factor in healing trauma is to personally know that we are not alone... this is the cry of attachment pain, "Is anyone with me... am I alone?" Jesus never gives up on reaching her as Mike didn't, as He does with us, and I believe she'll never give up on them trusting they will be there for her."

Book One P1 – *Out of the Darkness: An Autobiography of Love*
Book One P2 – *Out of the Darkness: An Autobiography of Love*
Book Two - *Becoming Pearl: An Autobiography of Love*
Book Three - *The City of Hope: An Autobiography of Love*
Book Four – A journey still being written.

Introduction

Pearl by Jesus

My little one you are my Pearl of great price. I have brought you out of the darkness and out of great suffering to be my jewel, my precious and beloved child. That is who you are and will always be. You will show others what it means to be a child of the king my little one. You will show them how loved and precious they are to me no matter what this world has taught them about who they are. You will show them the truth. I will take all of your pain my little one and all of your tears and I will use them to bring hope and joy to those who need it the most.

I will send you out my little one to those who are lost in the darkness, to my hidden children who do not know what it is to be loved or wanted. Your story will give them hope and through you they will see and understand that they too are loved and wanted. You will show the world who I am through the things that I have shown you my little one and through the person that you are. You will show them the truth about what it means to be a child, a true child of God. My little one you will know what it is to love and be loved. I will give you a heart that is open and free. Free to love those I give to you and free to be loved also.

You will teach others how to reach out to those who have been hurt like yourself my little one, not only in your words but also in your actions. You will be a light for me in places where few other lights shine. I will give you a joy that will shine out to those around you bringing hope and life to those who have not known either. My little one you will be my blessing and my gift to this world, a jewel in my crown. You know what it is to suffer my little one, but you will also know what it is to dance with joy. You will love me with all of your heart and follow wherever I will lead you and when all is said and done and I take you home to be where I am, you will be glad that you lived the life I had for you my little one. Though the cost is very high you will say that it was worth it. All this and more will be true of you my little one, because you are my Pearl... and this is who I have made you to be.

Preface by Pearl

I wrote these books because Jesus asked me to do it. He asked me to because he wants to show you who he is and how much he loves his children. It will be difficult to read sometimes, the things I talk about are real and painful. They are the truth of what happened to me, but it isn't the darkness he wants you to see so much as the light that shines in the darkness. I didn't hold back or hide what happened or my own pain and brokenness, because it's only when you see the darkness for what it is, it's impact and the difficulty of recovering from it that you can see the miracle of what Jesus has done in his healing of my heart. He wants you to see through my story what he is willing to do to bring his children out of the darkness into the light of his love. Whether you have been hurt like me or not, we all need Jesus to go into the broken places and bring his light and his healing. We all need to know that we are loved and safe, always.

I hope that you will continue to read even when it is difficult and painful, because it is in those places we meet Jesus and see him most clearly for who he is. Don't be afraid because he is right there with you as you are reading, ready to bring life and hope and healing to your heart just like he did for me. His love for you isn't any less, his truth is the same for you as it is for me. He is with you and loves you just as you are, and he knows who you can be, who he made you to be, which is more than you can imagine right now. He is faithful to walk alongside you and lead you forward as you say yes to him, even if your yes is very small to begin with, he will take it and work through it to draw you closer to him.

My story may seem extraordinary to you and parts of it are hard to believe or understand... but see it as the beginning of a journey to discovering more of who Jesus is. Allow yourself to question and to wonder. Give yourself time to ponder on his words which aren't just for me but are his gift to all of us. He is with us on our journey drawing us forward towards his heart of love for us. This is just another step, one that I hope you will be willing to take.

Chapter 1

The Journey Makes the Destination Possible

I had reached the city of my promise, the City of Hope. It had been a long, long journey to get there and mostly I had doubted that I ever would. Even though I had reached the gates the battle with doubt and with despair continued. I remembered the Israelites in the desert. Jesus had led them out of captivity and darkness just like he has me. They had overcome many things, seen the enemy defeated, witnessed miracle after miracle but they hadn't made it to the Promised Land. Not yet. Their journey had brought them to the desert, not what they had been promised, not what they were expecting, not what they wanted. They were disappointed. They didn't understand. They wondered what was the point of everything they had been through to just to get there, why didn't you leave us in Egypt they asked? I have been like them a lot of the time. This is my desert. The in-between place, free of the past but not yet in the Promised Land. It's right there…. but I am still here in the desert and every time I think it is time, every time I move towards the promise it seems to disappear like a mirage in the sand and all I am left with is more desert stretching ahead of me. That has happened to me so many times. So what do I do? Do I turn away like the Israelites did or will I be like Joshua and say that the promise is still there for the taking, if only I stay willing and trust in who God is.

All through our healing journey with Jesus he has talked to us about the path he has for us. It is a spiritual path made up of many paths all woven together to make *the* path, the one that he has for us to follow. Like most spiritual things it can be a bit hard to understand sometimes but there is a purpose and a direction to the path. It is leading somewhere, and Jesus is the one who directs our steps along it, if we will follow him. Our choices determine the route the path takes and how long it needs to be. It is the journey which makes the destination possible. The path that takes us to our destination gives us everything that we will need when we get there. If we don't follow Jesus and his path for us we can't ever reach the destination he planned for us because it is only in following him and walking with him along the path that he made for each of us that we can go where he wants to take us. We may never reach that destination because of the choices we make but Jesus is always seeking to lead us there.

My little one I have been preparing you for many years now, even before you began to remember or even discover who you were. The preparation for all that I am calling you to, began long before all of that my little one. When I said to you it is coming soon that is because you were almost at the point of seeing all that I had been preparing you for my little one. I did not start preparing you when you first became aware of who you are. I always knew who you were my little one and I have been preparing you for this for all of your life. You will soon see all that I have prepared you for my little one because discovering who you were came at the end of your time of preparation and not at the beginning.

Really?

Yes my little one. I have always known who you were and what I was calling you to do. I began preparing you for this long ago my little one. I did not wait. I have been using everything to make you ready.

That is hard to understand Jesus because it seems to me most of what happened before was destroying me.

But I have used all of that my little one and will continue to use it so that you can do and be everything that you were created to be. My dearest one I enabled you to survive in a way that would make it possible for you to fulfill everything that I have for you. I use all of it. Everything is being used to prepare you my little one.

As I look back over my life Jesus is helping me to see the path I've taken, to see it as he sees it, to see Him in it. I am starting to understand why he has allowed the things he has, why he has led me the way he has, why he asked me to make the choices and to I've the life that I have. Why he has healed me the way that he has and what I have learned along the way. I am starting to see that the path has given me just what I will need for the life that is ahead of me.

Jesus was, and is clear, that the path I have taken has given me everything I need for the future he has for me. It hasn't always been that clear to me though and I have struggled and fought with him about the path he chose for me but now as we sat at the city gates and looked back together, he showed me different paths I could have taken.

My little one look over there what do you see?

Fields, a river, a few trees.

Do you know what that is my little one?

No, it's not where the path is. We didn't come that way.

No my little one we didn't. What do you think that means my little one?

I suppose we could have come that way, it looks flat, easy going. Not like the rocky hilly path I came down.

Yes my little one that is so. There are many ways I could have brought you here. All of those ways would have been good but the way I brought you was the best way even if it was not the easiest. My little one the life you are living is difficult and it is painful in many ways for you but it has taught you to depend on me for everything. It has set your heart on me and my way for you, over and above anything you might want apart from that. It has taught you many things about who you are and about who I have made you to be. It has helped you to trust me and hold on to me. It has made you ready my little one for the life that will be given to you. My dearest little one you are my beloved child. You are my Pearl. I know everything you need and everything that you want. It is in my heart to give you good things my little one, things which will make your heart sing with joy. Trust me to do so. I know who you are my little one.

Why is it dark over to the left and kind of foggy?

That is another path you could have taken my little one, the path of disobedience and pain.

I don't understand how can that be a path you have in your heart for me.

No my little one but it is the path you would have had to take if you had not been obedient and trusted me in everything. My dearest one it has always been my intention to bring you here and there are many paths you could have taken to reach this place. The best path is the path of trust and obedience my little one, which is difficult and painful I know, but it has brought you here by the straightest path, able to see and understand the path you were taking. Disobedience leads to a different path my little one. One that is much more difficult and painful because you cannot see, the path is obscured from your sight and you travel in darkness for the most part. It is not that I could not have brought you here by another path my little one but you chose the best path, the one that has helped you to become all that you can be.

But if I was disobedient how could I ever get here?

It would have taken much longer my little one and though you may have reached this point the city we could have given you would not have been the same.

3

So does the path determine the city?

Yes my little one it does. The city is the destination at the end of the path. If the path is to prepare you for what lies ahead then the path must determine what is at the end my little one.

I suppose that is true. So why can I see those paths, the long out easier one on the right and the dark disobedient one on the left and my path in the middle?

Because I am showing them to you my little one so that you can understand why I asked you to walk the path that I did.

So that you can give me the city that you want because only this path would prepare me for this city.

Yes my little one that is so.

So if I didn't come by this path there would be people you had for me to reach that I wouldn't.

Yes my little one.

That is kind of serious Jesus.

Yes my little one it is. My dearest one do not underestimate the importance of your choices but neither be burdened by them. Remember that I work all things for good. I am helping you to see and understand that you have walked a good path with me and that the city you have received is because of that my little one.

Well I'm glad Jesus. I haven't walked perfectly. None of us did. I still don't but you know that. I don't know what else to say about it except keep helping me cos I need it.

I know you do my little one.

The destination at the end of this path is the City of Hope but it is more than that because my path doesn't end here. Now that I've reached the city my path has a new purpose and a new destination. My true destination can only be found in Jesus and through him. It is to be who he created me to be. To do the things he planned for me to do, which I can only do if I am who he made me to be.

My dearest one the path that you are on leads only to one place, it leads to me my little one. I am your destination. I am all that you are hoping for and all that you will ever need. I will make it possible for you to walk this path my little one and to reach the destination that I have for you. That is my will and my purpose for you my little one.

Yes. I suppose it is. Jesus there is so much for me to learn and so far for me to go and so much healing to be done.

But it is all part of your journey my little one and I will use all of it to

accomplish my purposes for your life. It is not about the destination my little one but it is about the journey that you must take to reach it. The destination is that same for all of my children my little one but the journey that each of you must take is very different. It is the journey which sees the fulfillment of your calling and the purpose that I have for your life. Do not be anxious my little one about all that there is for you to do. Take one day at a time, for each journey is made up of the steps that are taken my little one. Each one is important and necessary. Each step leads to the next.

I can only be who I am made to be in partnership with Jesus. I can't do it alone. That's not how I'm made. Even Jesus could only be who he was with the Holy Spirit and the father. So being who I am means being one with him and allowing him to express himself through me, a unique expression of who he is. That is who he made me to be, a unique expression of who he is. His plans and purposes for me in this life are only part of this because Jesus lives in the eternal but here in this life, he has plans for me, things that he can only accomplish through me.

For we are God's handiwork, created in Christ Jesus to do good works, which God prepared in advance for us to do.
Ephesians 2:10 NIV

Before he started to heal us, before we even knew we needed his healing, or that it was us and not just Jennifer, he began talking to us about his promises, about his plans and his purposes. Jesus always knew of course that he would be able to give me so much more than had been taken. That he could take me on a path that would lead to healing even from the things I had suffered and that through it he could show me the truth about who he is and who I am, about what is real and what matters. That because of the path he had for me he would be able to take me places I would never have gone otherwise, teach me things I would never have learned, enable me to do what I could never have done and be the me that he always intended I should be. His path was from the beginning made to bring me here and from here lead me on into the future he has promised me. Seeing his purpose in the path, right from the beginning gives me hope for the future.

March 2007 A vision

I'm standing on a very small raft facing Jesus, holding on to Him. We are in the middle of a river, the water is cold and laps over the side of the raft which seems in danger of sinking. The water gets rougher and the sky darker. I wrap my arms around Him and He holds me tight. He tells me to open my eyes and look around. I let go a little, trusting Him to hold me and I look around. There is a storm raging. The water is very rough, the sky is full of black clouds and lightning is flashing. Jesus shows me all this- He's not perturbed and in the distance there is a small patch of blue sky and sunshine. The raft runs aground on a very small beach. We climb a grassy bank and look down into a valley where I can see thousands of lights- a vast city. We make our way down to it. The buildings are tall and dark, the streets are dark. We make our way into the city until we come to a church, an old church with the feel of a castle with a drawbridge. It is lit up and seems to be on a small hill. We go inside. It smells like an old church and looks like an old church. I fall to the floor as the power of the Spirit hits me. I look up at Jesus. He and the Spirit are embracing, communing, perfect unity, perfect joy. The Spirit intertwines and envelops Jesus in golden light which shimmers (this is the most beautiful thing I have ever seen). Jesus reaches down and pulls me in. The golden light fades but now we are moving as one. I am in Jesus and He is in me and there is no distinction. People start to stream into the church through many doors. They are covered in grey blankets. They are coming to Jesus/me. As we touch them the grey blankets fall away and there is light, light in their faces. I see light spreading from the church, throughout the whole city which is now light and full of life and joy.

Jesus has given me lots of visions, prophetic words and dreams all telling me about the future he has planned for me. I see many of his promises and the journey I have taken in this one vision. The storm that takes me to the place he wants me to be as I cling to him. His plan to bring light and hope to those who are in darkness. His desire to be one with me, for us to work together to bring light and life to those who need it the most, to draw people to him, to bring hope to the church. All of these things and more he has planned for me. All of them are part of the destination he has for me. Understanding the destination has helped draw us along the path even when we haven't really understood the purpose of what was being asked. It can be hard to see what the path is giving you at the time.

Knowing the direction and purpose of the path still means trusting Jesus to lead you in the way that is best, often it has seemed like the path he was leading me on was going in the opposite direction, leading me away from the promise instead of towards it.

I am sorry... crying.

I know you are my little one. My dearest one the enemy is tormenting you with his lies but that is what they are. Your future is in my hands my little one. I know that what I am asking of you is hard but that does not mean that it is bad. It does not mean that my promises will never come. It does not mean that I have lied my little one.

No. When you say it like that I see it Jesus. But I don't want to do this job. I don't want to be here. I don't want to be Jennifer I don't want to be a grown up I don't want to be alone anymore and there is no escape from all of that and even if I am better than I was, all that seems to happen is more of the things I don't want and it is hard to bear Jesus. It seems like you don't love me and that that the things you've said aren't true… crying.

I know how it seems my little one but that is not how it is. It takes faith to follow where I lead my little one. Often it will seem like I am leading you away from the things that I have promised you but that is not so my little one. It is only that I know the best way for you. The way that will help you draw closer to me and become all that I have made you to be. My dearest one if I ask you to trust me it is because trust is necessary my little one. You cannot go where I am taking you without trust.

Because everything I see will tell me I am going the wrong way.

Yes my little one often it will.

It is hard to keep on trusting Jesus when I seem to be going in the wrong direction for years and years.

I know it is my little one.

I don't think I can do this Jesus… crying.

But you can my little one. I would not ask it of you otherwise.

I know I just need to trust you and keep walking forward with you even if I don't like where you are taking me but I am tired and I am scared and I just want it to be over. I want to see your promises Jesus. I don't know how much longer I can keep doing this… crying.

My little one all the days of your life I have watched over you dreaming of all you can be in this world. You are my child my little one and I love you beyond anything you can imagine. Everything that is mine belongs to you

my little one and can never be taken from you. The time you have in this life is so short my little one but it can accomplish great things if you surrender it to me. I know my dearest one that life has not been kind to you and that you often wish that it would end but it is not yet time my little one. My promises will come and when they do you will see that I have led you this way for a reason. You will see that I am well able to do everything I have said. You will see that I can take your suffering and use it for great good my little one and even though the cost has been so very high you will not regret it. These things are hard for you to see right now my little one and that is why you must trust me. Trust is necessary my little one because you cannot see. Do not trust what you see my little one trust only in me and in who I am. I will not fail you. I will be with you in every moment and even though the path is hard I will sustain you on it and give you all that you need. Keep going my little one. Do not listen to lies but hold on to my hand and allow me to lead you forward into the life that I have promised you many times. It is not a lie my little one. It is real and true just as I am real and true and everything I am asking of you is to make it possible for you to live this life my little one. So that you will be strong enough and will not crumble and fall when opposition comes. So that you will know who you are and who I am also when others question and doubt. I am asking this of you because it is necessary my little one. Not because I do not love you but because I do. Keep trusting my little one. Keep hoping. I am with you helping you. Keep your eyes fixed on me and do not listen to lies. Everything I have for you is good my little one. My promises are true and will be fulfilled. There is nothing to fear.

Mostly I haven't liked the path and didn't see the point of it. Trusting in Jesus' sight is the only way to walk the path he has for us...He has taught me this in so many ways. He sees what I don't see. He understands what I don't understand. If we follow him closely, he can lead us on the straightest path. If we turn aside, go astray, do our own thing, the path has to be longer, twisting and turning, to take us where we need to go.

Trust in the Lord with all your heart
and lean not on your own understanding;
in all your ways submit to him, and
he will make your paths straight.

Proverbs 3:5-6

Chapter 2

The Gift of the Path

Jesus put the destination in my heart from the beginning. When I was born, I was whole, one person. Jesus gave me everything I needed to grow into the person he made me to be. Like a garden my heart was planted with good seeds, everything he wanted me to be and everything he wanted me to do and he looked on me with joy and with love because of who I am. He was never ashamed of me. Never wished I didn't exist or saw me as a mistake or an inconvenience. He saw me through eyes that loved what they saw, not for any other reason except that I was me. He wanted good things for me. He wanted me to grow and learn and become all the things he had for me to become. He had good dreams for my life even before it began. He celebrated me then and he celebrates me now.

He showed me how true this was in a way that I could never forget, in a way that touched my heart and stayed with me because I know it was and is the truth of how he sees me.

I will try to remember everything that happened, but I was crying a lot. I was in Jesus arms, but Angels came, first they made sure my shoes of hope were on my feet properly then they covered me with something silver and sparkly and then they wrapped me up in something pink and sparkly a bit like a cocoon with just my face showing. Jesus said it was to keep me safe, from myself I suppose. Then he put his hand over my heart and something golden came out of him and into me. Hope maybe. So, I was held and safe and I couldn't run away. Jesus carried me from daddy's room of comfort into a different room. It was warm and dark and pink, and it made me think of a womb. I think that's what it was. Jesus started to talk to me about how they had thought of me and planned me. How they had wanted me to be me. And there were lots of pictures being kind of projected onto the walls. And he told me they were the dreams they had for my life when they were making me. And I knew how much they loved and wanted me, and it made me cry and cry. I am not sure if the womb place was really in daddy's heart because of what came next. Jesus carried me out into a bright light, and I knew that I had been born and I was snatched out of Jesus arms and I knew that was when the bad things were happening, but I didn't see them. And Jesus was there with me. He never left me.

Then we were in a different place. A dark place and I saw Jesus on the cross and he was bleeding and he was looking at me and I knew he was saying that this is how much he wanted me. And it was how much daddy wanted me and the Holy Spirit too. They wanted me so much and loved me so much that they went through that so that they could rescue me and save me, and I could be theirs. And I cried and cried. And then I was in Jesus arms again and he laid me on a stone table all wrapped up in my bundle. It made me think of sacrifices and I was a bit scared. And daddy was there and the Holy Spirit too. They were all stood around me and Jesus was holding a golden knife over me and I got scared that maybe it was the enemy but then I remembered about Abraham and Isaac so I decided I would trust them and see what happened. Jesus took the knife, but he didn't hurt me. He cut through the pink stuff and the silver stuff and under that I could see thick black cords wrapped round me. He cut those too and the moment he did I jumped up and into his arms and cried and cried because I knew I was free and that I was loved. And I was crying and I was thinking, I am not sure why, about how ugly I am, on the outside anyway, in my fat old body but then I saw me in Jesus arms with my pretty dress and my crown of love and my shoes of hope and my long shiny hair and my freckles and I saw that I am a beautiful princess really and not ugly at all. And I cried because that is how they see me, how I really am. And Jesus carried me to his throne and sat me on his knee. And he was saying how I wasn't less than any of his children. I was right there with him, not left out, not forgotten, not second best. And I cried a lot. And then it was like there was a river going into me. It was golden and sparkly but kind of like water too and it was full of rainbows and I knew that they were pouring their love in to fill up the hole in my heart. And I cried and cried and that was the end.

The bad things that happened to me meant that to reach the destination he has for me the path would not only have to heal and set me free from the past but restore everything that was taken and lost. A path that would take me to the destination he had for me would be long and hard and painful because of everything that would be needed so that I can be who he created me to be.

The purpose he has for my life, the plans and promises he has told me about, come out of who I am in him. They are part of who he made me to be, put there in the beginning with all the other good things he put in my heart. To fulfil these plans, I will need to know who Jesus is, to know him and his character, his love for me, to know my need of him. I will need to let him into my heart completely, to be one with him, to be like Jesus in his obedience to the father and his dependence on the Holy Spirit. I will need to know the truth about reality, true reality and what that means. I will need to be able to live out of the spirit, in obedience to the spirit, to hear him, to follow him.

Jesus has not only planned for me to share my story of healing with others but to bring the truths of the kingdom and the spiritual realties that go with that to his children, his church.

I have been teaching you how to live in the spiritual world, in the true reality my little one where things can be seen for what they truly are. This is a picture for all of my children. All of you live in two worlds my little one but so many of my children never really see or understand this. I want you to open their eyes to the true reality which is all around them and within them. I want them to understand who they are as my children. I want you to be the story my little one.

So the story of my healing is a gateway to something more. To teach your children about the spiritual world, about you and about who they are. And I do that I suppose by being me and living the way you want us all to live.

Yes my little one just so.

But I think I have a long way to go in that Jesus with so much more to learn. I still get caught up in thinking this world is the one that matters, which is why I get so depressed sometimes.

I know my little one.

And that is why this is taking so long because it's not just about telling a story of what you've done but of who you are and who we are, which means I need to learn it for myself and learn to live in it.

Yes my little one.

I am going to be here forever.

No my little one you are not. You are learning and growing far more than you realize. I am helping you my little one so that you are able to help my children go where I want them to go and be who I have called them to be. This is a great calling my little one and I have been preparing you for many years, but it is not endless my dearest one. You will be ready to begin walking with me through the city helping those I give to you not just to heal and find the freedom that you have but also to live in the true reality that is the kingdom. This is more than you have understood my little one and I want you to see it before we begin.

I had a picture which helps me understand. It was a wave coming up the beach, like when the tide turns, and it starts coming in. The first wave pushes its way up the beach and it's kind of slow maybe but then the second waves kind of rides on that one and goes much faster and further than the first wave. The first wave is the books and the second wave is this kingdom stuff.

My little one what I will ask of you will come from the books, the opposition to the first wave is great my little one. The enemy will put all of his efforts into preventing the books from ever being published because once the first wave comes the second one will follow, and it is the second one he fears even more than the first.

Why?

Because my dearest one you have been given the keys to open the secrets of the kingdom and you are not only going to share those secrets but also to give those keys to others. That is dangerous to him my little one. The kingdom of darkness does not want those keys to be released to those who are faithful to me.

I think you might need to explain that more Jesus.

My little one I have given you access to the things of the kingdom. I have taken you to places and shown you things to help you understand not only your own journey but who you are in me. My children need to understand who they are my little one because once they do there is nothing that can stand in their way. They will live out of that truth my little one and be all that they can be in me. The enemy fears this because his greatest weapon is to convince my children that they cannot do and be all that I say.

Is it?

Yes my little one it is. My children were made for so much more than to go to church once a week or even to serve me in their everyday lives. My children are meant to live out of the truth of who they are my little one, which changes everything. As I show them who they are they can become more than they ever dreamed they could be and do all that I created them for. They can live out the purpose that I have hidden in their heart my little one. They cannot do it otherwise.

You always said I would show people who you are Jesus, but you want them to know who they are as well. That has been such a big part of my journey. It still is.

Yes my little one it is.

To be all that he made me to be and to fulfil my purpose I will need to be unshakable, to know that I am safe and loved and wanted, for Jesus to be my bigger reality over and above what I see and experience in the outside world. To be able to stand in the face of everything that the world and the enemy will bring against me. I will need to know who I am, as his child first and foremost and then as his servant. I will need to be able to stand in the truth of who I am, to know I am who he says I am and not shaken by anyone else

12

saying whatever about me or believes about me just as Jesus did. He trusted who his father said he was even when the whole world mocked him and hung him on a cross, he was unshakeable.

Jesus plans for me to share all I have learned about the things of the spirit and the kingdom and about who are in him has meant that my path has taken me to many different places in the spirit. In a lot of ways, it has been much more of an inside journey than an outside one. I've found that hard and haven't understood it a lot of the time. I have spent a lot of time asking him to change things on the outside when he was wanting to change things on the inside and teach me about the true reality of life. He has been very patient.

I can't fulfil the plans he has for me alone. Almost from the beginning Jesus has made it clear that I would work hand in hand with daddy Mike. He is part of my promise and it is together that we will do all the things that Jesus has told me about and prepared me for. The path that I have taken has given me a relationship with daddy Mike that is centered completely on Jesus. He hasn't let me depend on my daddy for my healing or my faith or for anything else. All of it has come directly from Jesus or the Holy Spirit or from daddy God. He has led me down a path where I had to trust in who Jesus told me daddy Mike was, because often, I couldn't see it for myself. Trusting him was made very difficult, not just because of the physical distance between us, but by the enemy who has worked hard to separate us.

This has been the path I have taken, one which was made especially for me to give me everything that I will need to be me, with everything that means, and to fulfil the plans and purposes Jesus has for my life.

My little one what do I want for you more than anything?
That I would be who you made me to be. That I would know who you are and who I am.

Yes my little one and do you think it is easy for you to receive these things in a world that opposes my will in every way?
No.

No my little one it is not. In order for you to be who you were made to be you must first know who I am and who you are also. This comes not through all the good and lovely things that you want my little one but through the struggles and pain of this life. That is not because I want it so my little one only because to take hold of all that I want to give to you, you must be strong enough for the battles that will come. You must be healed enough to be able to accept everything I want to give to you.

13

You must be free enough to walk in my strength and not your own. I know my dearest one that you are weary and do not really understand the path you are on but hold on to me. Keep your eyes fixed on me my little one. It is not for nothing. Everything you are going through is reaping a reward both for you and for others. I am with you. I will not ever leave you. You are my beloved child and you are loved and wanted in this life and in the one that is to come. Let that be enough for you my little one. When it is hard hold on to me. When the darkness closes in draw even closer. This world is a painful and difficult place my little one but you are not alone in it. I know who you are my little one. I will not forget my promises to you. I am making a way for you to be everything you were created to be. Hold on and trust me. I am everything you need.

"I have told you these things,
So that in me you may have peace.
In this world you will have trouble.
But take heart! I have overcome the world."

John 16:33

Chapter 3
The Path of Suffering

It seems to me my path is made up two of different strands. There is the path Jesus allowed and the path that he planned. At times I have struggled to understand and accept both of them. I have questioned my existence and why I had to live at all. Why didn't he just let me die? The very things that he allowed, the bad things, have caused me to ask the hard questions, to seek out the meaning and purpose of my life and to cling to the only one who had any of the answers. This was part of what he wanted to give to me, part of what I need, to understand clearly who I am, why I am me, why I exist. But I would only find out these answers if I was willing to seek, to seek with all my heart because my life depended on it. He worked through my pain to give me what I needed...meaning, purpose and a knowledge of who I truly am.

The people who hurt me, the things that were done to me, the things that I did and the enemy who tormented me, all told me who I was. They told me I was nothing and nobody, that I didn't deserve to live, that I shouldn't even exist. When it seems like your very existence was a mistake or a bad thing, when life seems to offer nothing but pain and fear, the question 'why' is asked over and over again. Why was I born? Why did I have to exist? Why did you allow the bad things to happen? Why didn't you stop it? Why didn't you let me die? The same questions over and over again. It has taken time for Jesus to answer them in a way I can understand. It has taken time and a lot of healing. They aren't easy questions and they don't have easy answers.

Job asked the same kind of questions in his suffering.

After this, Job opened his mouth and cursed the day of his birth. He said: "May the day of my birth perish, and the night that said, 'A boy is conceived!' That day may it turn to darkness; may God above not care about it; may no light shine on it. May gloom and utter darkness claim it once more; may a cloud settle over it; may blackness overwhelm it. That night —may thick darkness seize it; may it not be included among the days of the year nor be entered in any month. May that night be barren; may no shout of joy be heard in it. May those who curse days curse that day, those who are ready to rouse Leviathan. May its morning

stars become dark; may it wait for daylight in vain and not see the first rays of dawn, for it did not shut the doors of the womb on me to hide trouble from my eyes.

"Why did I not perish at birth, and die as I came from the womb? Why were there knees to receive me and breasts that I might be nursed? For now I would be lying down in peace; I would be asleep and at rest with kings and rulers of the earth, who built for themselves places now lying in ruins, with princes who had gold, who filled their houses with silver. Or why was I not hidden away in the ground like a stillborn child, like an infant who never saw the light of day? There the wicked cease from turmoil, and there the weary are at rest. Captives also enjoy their ease; they no longer hear the slave driver's shout. The small and the great are there, and the slaves are freed from their owners. "Why is light given to those in misery, and life to the bitter of soul, to those who long for death that does not come, who search for it more than for hidden treasure, who are filled with gladness and rejoice when they reach the grave? Why is life given to a man whose way is hidden, whom God has hedged in? Nor be entered in any of the months. May that night be barren; May no shout of joy be heard in it. May those who curse days curse that day, those who are ready to rouse Leviathan. May its morning stars become dark; may it wait for daylight in vain and not see the first rays of dawn, for it did not shut the doors of the womb on me to hide trouble from my eyes. "Why did I not perish at birth, and die as I came from the womb? Why were there knees to receive me and breasts that I might be nursed? For now I would be lying down in peace; I would be asleep and at rest with kings and rulers of the earth, who built for themselves places now lying in ruins, with princes who had gold, who filled their houses with silver. Or why was I not hidden away in the ground like a stillborn child, like an infant who never saw the light of day? There the wicked cease from turmoil, and there the weary are at rest. Captives also enjoy their ease; they no longer hear the slave driver's shout. The small and the great are there, and the slaves are freed from their owners. "Why is light given to those in misery, and life to the bitter of soul, to those who long for death that does not come, who search for it more than for hidden treasure, who are filled with gladness and rejoice when they reach the grave? Why is life given to a man whose way is hidden, whom God has hedged in? For sighing has become my daily food; my groans pour out like water. What I feared has come upon me; what I dreaded has happened to me.

16

I have no peace, no quietness;
I have no rest, but only turmoil."

Job 3 NIV

Job expresses the pain of his existence in a way I recognize. We have asked Jesus over and over why we had to live. I wasn't a planned child. I was a child born in shame, not celebrated. Being born always seemed like a bad thing to me. It meant I had to live a life that was mostly about pain and suffering. The day of my birth was like Job says, one that I have wished never existed, and with every birthday that comes around that it could be thrown into the sea and never seen again.

As if this wasn't enough that I believed my very existence was a bad thing, the cults took my birthday for their own, to celebrate my belonging to them, to Satan. To me it has been a bad day, full of darkness, bad memories of the things that were done to me and a deep shame from the belief that I gave myself to the enemy.

What do you want for this birthday Jesus? Eventually I mean. Not this one.

I want you to be at peace with it my little one. For it to be a day when you can celebrate all that I have done.

Crying ..But I don't want that Jesus. I don't want this and you together.

But I am in everything my little one. To keep me apart from this day would be to deny many things that I have given to you. So many things that I have and will do.

But I don't see you Jesus. To me it seems like their day. Not yours and not mine.

Every day is mine my little one. We will take back this day that they have stolen from you and it will be our day my little one and not theirs.

I don't want to.

Why my little one?

I don't want anything of theirs. It is dirty and wrong.

But it is not theirs my little one. They took it from you. It does not belong to them. My little one the more that you are able to see me in this day the more that you are able to take back what was stolen from you. You are not dirty my little one. You are clean for I have made you clean. You are new in me and nothing can ever change that. My little one it does not matter what they have taken from you for everything will be restored but you must be willing to accept my gift to you my

little one. I cannot force it on you nor would I wish to do so. It is my gift to you my little one. A brand new day just for you.

Why can't you give me another day?

But then what would happen to this day my little one. It would be forever in the hands of the enemy. My little one I do not want them to have anything that belongs to you. This is your day my little one and not theirs.

But I don't believe that. I don't want to celebrate them. I don't want to celebrate them.

My little one I know everything that was done to you on this day and everything that they forced you to do but that does not change my love for you my little one nor does it change your love for me. I am yours my little one and you are mine no matter what lies in the past. This is not their day my little one it is yours. My little one it is possible for you to see this day differently and for it to be a day of celebration rather than a day of pain.

Is it?

Yes my little one it is. I know my little one that you would rather I cast this day into the sea so that you need never look at it again but my dearest one that is not the way to overcome the fear or to heal the pain.

What is the way Jesus?

The way is found in who I am my little one. When you see who I am in this day then you can begin to accept the truth and be healed of the pain that you feel.

But it is a lot of days Jesus not just one cos it was every year and I don't know the truth about it. Not really.

But you know that it was a day given over to celebrating your life in them, your belonging and giving yourself to them.

Was it?

Yes my little one it was.

I don't remember.

Not fully my little one for many of the memories and their full meaning are still hidden from you but you understand, nevertheless.

I seem to but I don't know why.

Because even though the memories themselves are hidden my little one the truth of them is not. You know it in your heart.

How do I see you in that Jesus?

By remembering that you are mine. You were always mine my little one. Though they told you a lie that has remained hidden in your heart. You did not ever belong to them my little one. You are my child not theirs.

18

It was a lie.

Yes my little one it was.

And you never believed it Jesus…Crying.

No my little one for I saw the truth. I still see the truth my little one. You belong to me and nothing can ever take you from me.

But if I believed it doesn't it make it true?

No my little one the truth does not change just because you do not know what it is.

No. It just is.

Yes my little one. It just is.

So no matter what they did and no matter what I did that didn't change the truth.

No my little one it didn't.

And when you, when I see the truth and accept it then, it isn't their day anymore.

No my little one it is your day to celebrate that no matter what they did they could not take you from me. It is your day to celebrate that you are mine and will always be so.

Crying…That is a good thing to celebrate Jesus.

Yes my little one it is.

Seeing Jesus in this darkest of days is a picture of what he wants for my whole life. He wants me to see him in it, to see the truth so that I can be set free from the lies of the enemy and the pain and the fear that come with them. Jesus celebrates my existence. He planned me with joy and with love and no matter what this life has brought me that has never changed. It never will.

My little one you belong to us. You are a princess of the eternal kingdom. Everything here will pass my little one but these things will remain. My little one this is a day to remember who you truly are. Not how the world sees you my little one, not who they say that you are but who I say that you are. You are precious and you are loved. You are held so close to me my little one and you can never be taken away. Your father holds you in his arms and sings over you with delight my little one.

These things are real and true and eternal. They will not ever change. I know my little one that this world is a painful and difficult place for you to live in. I know what it is to be misunderstood my little one to be seen as someone you are not. I held on to my father in those times my little one and difficult as they were I knew there was a greater truth. A truth that could never be changed even if it could not be seen by those

around me. My little one you belong with me and even though you are here in this world you are always with me. My little one I am with you in everything I am with you now my little one. I do not ever leave you. You are safe and you are loved and there is nothing to fear my little one.

The answers to my questions of why are found in his love for me but that is hard to understand too. How does love allow such suffering? How can he say he loves me and still let those things happen to me? But then I think of the cross and all Jesus suffered there. He suffered because he knew what would come from it. His father allowed his son to suffer because of what would be accomplished. It is still hard to understand but it does mean that just because I have suffered doesn't mean I'm not loved.

My little one I have always loved you. I know my little one that my love is hard to see and understand at times. To you it seems like often I have not loved you, not in the way that you understand love or the way that you want to be loved. My little one my love is deeper than you know. It will take you to places that you cannot imagine. It will bring you life and healing and hope. But my little one it will not make your life easy or painless. My father loved me my little one just as he loves you but my life here on this earth was full of pain and it was not ever easy my little one for many reasons. The pain and suffering you have endured and continue to endure does not mean that you are not loved my little one. It means that you were born into a world that is full of sin that has turned away from me and is broken. That is why you have suffered my little one not because I do not love you. My love will restore everything that has been lost to you my little one but not in the way that you expect or want. I will do it in the best way for you my little one so that you can be everything you were created to be. I know my little one that the road is hard and long and you have yet to see anything of my promises to you but that does not mean that they are not real or true only that you have yet to see them. I am healing you my little one so that you will be ready for the life that I am giving to you. You could not live it otherwise my little one. You could not do or be any of the things I have planned for you. Healing must come and is coming. I know my little one that my ways seem unkind to you at times but I am never unkind my little one. What seems unkind to you is really my loving kindness poured out, enabling you to walk a path that would otherwise be impossible for you. This path will take you into the life I have for you my little one and that is why I say it is a good path. Not because it is easy or painless but because it leads to life and hope and joy and all of the things that you are dreaming of. I know my little one that this is hard for you to see and that your pain is overwhelming at times but I am with you my little one. You do not ever walk alone. Even though the cost is very great and there are other easier paths you could have taken this is the one that I chose for you. I know who you are and though your suffering is very great I know the reward that is waiting for you. It is not your reward only my little one it is mine for we share in everything you and I. I am making a way for you to become everything that I created you to be. No matter what the enemy has done or will do I am far greater my little one. There is nothing he can do to stop my plans for you.

There is hope my little one though you do not yet see it. I am waiting to pour it out into your life my little one and through you to many others who have also had their hope taken from them. My little one, my dearest little one you are not forgotten or abandoned. There is nothing that can take you from me. I am your hope and your strength. I know the things that you are longing for my little one but I must make you ready so that when they are given you are able to accept them. It would not help you my little one to give you the things you need or want before you are able to do this. I know my little one that the fullness of my plan is still hidden from you. You have yet to fully understand even the things that I have revealed to you but I have so much more for you than you know. This time will make it possible for you to be and do everything I have planned for you my little one. It will come and when it does you will see and understand so much more than you do now why I chose this path for you. My little one hold on to me and do not let go. Do not let the pain you feel keep you from me. I am your healer my little one and everything that you need. I am making you new so that you can be who you were created you to be. Do not fear this my little one though it will be a life that is strange to you I have made you perfect to live it out with me. My little one you are so very loved.

All that I have placed in your heart, all the hopes and dreams that you are still so afraid to see will be fulfilled my little one. They are my hopes and dreams for you my little one. They are not bad things. They are the things that are waiting for you along the path that we travel together. My little one I am holding you and loving you. I will make you whole in me my little one and able to take hold of all the hope that I am

21

giving to you. Hope which will enable you to walk forward with me into all that I have planned for you. This is not the end my little one it is only the beginning. Hold on then my little one and keep trusting. I am with you. I will not ever leave you. I am sure and I am certain just as the hope I have for you is sure and certain. I will not fail you my little one. I will help you to see the hope I have for you in time my little one but for now hold on to me and trust in my love for you. A love which is healing all the hurts of the past my little one so that you can be all that you were created to be. My little one you were created for so much more than this. Do not despair then my little one though the promise seems far away to you it is not. It is only just ahead of you. Keep holding on my little one. I am with you.

As we have spent time with Jesus he helped me to see and understand these things more like he does. We have all questioned his love and his path for us but he has always been patient in helping us to understand more.

There was purpose in allowing Jesus to suffer and there was purpose in allowing me to suffer too. Jesus has spent many hours talking to me about this, to help me understand his purpose in allowing my suffering, his purpose for my life. How even the things that have happened to me, and what it has taken to recover, can be worth the pain.

Hi Jesus.

Hello my little one.

I suppose I need your help with the things I am thinking Jesus. I feel sad but maybe I am seeing something.

Tell me what you see my little one.

That I am here for a reason. That you must have a good reason for keeping me alive because you love me and even if it is hard for me to believe sometimes it does matter to you if I suffer. Sometimes I think it can't matter because if it did you wouldn't let me keep on suffering. But I think maybe that part is wrong.

My little one every tear you cry is precious to me. Your suffering has been very great my little one and all of it matters. That does not mean my little one that it is what I wanted for you but it does mean that I allowed it. I allowed it because I understand what you do not. That all the suffering you have endured will be used to drive back the kingdom of darkness and to keep others from suffering as you have. More than that my little one it will keep a great many of my children from the eternal suffering that they would otherwise have endured. My dearest

one such suffering is far greater than anything than even you have endured. I do not want that for any of my children. I have paid a great price my little one so that they do not have to and I have asked you to pay that price with me my little one, to share in all of my sufferings so that my children might be rescued and brought in from the darkness.

I know it mattered that you suffered Jesus. It mattered to you because you cried about it and were afraid and struggled to accept it and I know it mattered to daddy because he loves you but you still suffered Jesus. I suppose in some ways you still do because you are with us all in our suffering. I suppose accepting that suffering is somehow necessary to follow you, like you said to share in your sufferings. I suppose that is what it means to be one with you and maybe the closer we are to you the more we will suffer I don't know because it is hard to imagine I could suffer more than I have. But I see that suffering is part of what it means to belong to you somehow, in this world. Maybe that helps me accept it better without believing the lie that it doesn't matter to you and you don't care. We suffer together Jesus. Don't we?

Yes my little one we do. I know my little one that it is a hard thing to accept. I know that your heart is still hurting and longing for an end to all the suffering, not only yours my little one but the suffering of all my children but my little one my heart is also hurting and longing for the suffering to end. That is what we are doing my little one. We are working together with all of my children who are willing, to bring all of the suffering and pain of this world to an end not because it doesn't matter my little one but because it does.

Yes. I think I see that and accepting that my suffering is part of that somehow, part of working towards it all ending. Kind of using it against itself, if I give it to you and let you use it, well you can make it count. You can somehow move towards ending the suffering. I don't know Jesus. But maybe accepting suffering past and present and future and not being afraid of it or trying to escape from it is part of surrendering it to you. Or maybe it is all about surrendering to you no matter if it means suffering, accepting that it will and not being afraid but knowing it all works for good, for ending suffering, I don't know. I suppose it takes the fear out of the future.

Yes my little one it does. Acceptance of suffering will help set you free from many things my little one. Not because I want you to suffer but because I do not want you to be controlled by your fear of it.

Well knowing that you are with me in it, that you are in control and that you care, that you use it all and it all works towards ending suffering and that the suffering will end. For me it will Jesus. I know that those who are lost, that is hard to understand, eternal suffering. But I know you don't want it. I don't understand why it's a thing if you don't want it but maybe that is a big question that I will ask another time. For now it is about accepting my own suffering in this life and not being afraid of it. Trusting that you do care and you suffer with me and that you are and will use it all to end the suffering of others and that it is part of what it means to share in your suffering and to belong to you in this world. Something like that.

Yes my little one. Acceptance of suffering in this world is difficult my little one for yourself and others. Acceptance does not mean that it does not matter or that you do not want it to end only that you are not afraid of it.

Yes because then it doesn't have any power over me does it. It can't control me. It sets me free.

Yes my little one exactly so.

Which is what you are doing. Setting me free from fear.

Yes my little one it is.

You always do things in a way I don't expect Jesus.

I know my little one but I will always do what I have promised.

Accepting that suffering is part of life and most especially part of belonging to and following Jesus was something I have needed to learn not only to set me free from the fear that was holding me but to set me free to live the life he has for me, not controlled by the fear of what might be but trusting in his goodness and in his strength to bring me through. Not being afraid to suffer because I know that there is purpose in it all.

Suffering is a hard thing to accept though. Sometimes it has seemed to me that suffering is all there is in life, that it has overwhelmed everything else. When we died, age 5 and went to heaven, just for a moment, Jesus sent us back knowing what we would suffer, knowing everything that was ahead for us.

I have been back into the memory of the marriage with the Goatman two more times. Yesterday in the memory the Goatman was doing it to me and saying over and over you belong to me you belong to me and I was saying back I belong to you. I saw blackness surrounding me and going into me. It was very horrible. Jesus held me and rocked me and I was surrounded by golden rainbows. He held me close and it was like I was going into his heart. It is hard to describe but that's how it felt. I did cry a lot. Today the Goatman threw me to the crowd. I don't know how many

24

there were. It seemed like a lot. They grabbed me and carried me away. I was laid on my back. I knew what they were doing to me and I had my mouth covered so I couldn't move or make a sound but I hardly felt it. I was staring up at the trees and the sky. The trees were just branches with no leaves and the sky was full of twinkling stars that I watched. They twinkled and twinkled. Jesus said he made them twinkle just for me so I could look at them and not really know what was happening to me. I held on to him and cried and cried. It was very terrible even though I was looking at the twinkling stars. I could kind of hear the laughing and screaming and voices but they seemed far away. So that is what is happening. I have been wondering a lot if there is any hope for me. I know I need to look at Jesus and not what is happening but it is hard to do that all the time. I asked him to make himself very big to me so I can't see anything else.

That part of the memory was terrible. It wasn't a new memory but part of one that we had right back at the beginning when Jennifer had been on the outside. But this time I saw it differently. I saw the next part differently too and in some ways this was even harder to accept.

The memory began where it left off. I was laid on the grass. That was all I could see grass and mud. I couldn't move or feel anything like I wasn't connected to the body. There were no people anywhere. I don't know where they went. But then I was surrounded by darkness. Demons. They were laughing and saying they had come to take me because I belonged to them. I couldn't move or speak. But I saw that they were held back and couldn't get me. Like there was an invisible wall. Then the wall seemed to be more visible. A golden shimmery wall. The more I looked at it the clearer it got. I saw that the four Angels were stood in a circle around me. They had their backs to me so they were facing the demons. They spread out their wings so they overlapped and made a barrier so I was completely protected. The place where I was seemed to fill with a golden light and I knew I was in heaven. Jesus was in front of me. I was still on the ground and couldn't move. He said, 'my child' and he bent down and kissed me on the forehead. I knew he was bringing me back to life. Jesus faded, heaven faded, the Angels faded and I was left alone on the grass. Grandad came and picked me up. That was the end. I cried and cried because I didn't want to be back I wanted to be in heaven. It was so wonderful. Even remembering it made me not want to leave. But he brought me back. He brought me back knowing what would happen. And it seemed like he left me there even though I know he didn't. I suppose at the time it was how it seemed. I cried so much.

It took me a long time to understand and even forgive Jesus for sending me back into the life that was waiting for me, knowing what would happen for me. Jesus accepted his suffering because of what would be accomplished through it. Is it different for us? I don't think so. If we are hidden in Christ, we are one with him, we share in his life and in his suffering for the sake of his children. I don't think he sent us back for our sake, or mine. We belonged to him in that moment. He sent us back as his child, one with him. Back into a life of pain and suffering because of all that he would accomplish through it. That was our path even then, my path which led me here to this place, to the city of my promise. A promise that was put in my heart from the very beginning but not revealed to me for many years. I didn't understand. How could I? Everything was broken. Everything was pain. The truth was hidden by lies and by fear. So much fear. It took a long time for me to be able to see the truth, to see my life from a different viewpoint, to see it through Jesus eyes. Suffering overwhelmed me, it broke me, but it didn't destroy me. I was held, I was safe. I was given everything I needed to survive. Though the suffering has lasted many years I was always safe. I never knew it. I didn't feel it but it was and is the truth. Suffering doesn't change the truth, but it can make it harder to see and accept.

The truth was that I was never alone no matter how it felt to me, that I was never abandoned even though it seemed like I was. It took time and a lot of healing to see and accept this was true. When I was locked in the box or buried under the ground Jesus was with me, holding me, helping me. When I was being hurt or tortured, he gave me the strength to endure. When I was so, so alone and afraid he was right there with me.

So every part of my story had a purpose?
Yes my little one it does.
And you will help me find that purpose?
Yes my little one I will. My little one there is much treasure that I have hidden in the story I have given you.
Oh, treasure in the darkness.
Yes my little one. It is there for you to discover as you learn how to see with my eyes and not your own.
But the pain and the fear and the darkness get in the way Jesus.
Yes my little one they do but as you are healed and the hidden things are brought out into the light I will help you to see the treasure that is hidden there my little one.
I need to be looking for it.
Yes my little one you do. I will help you.
I suppose maybe, this treasure is revealing who you are. That is because you are our treasure.
Yes my little one I am your treasure. I have hidden myself in every part of your story ready for you to find my little one. I am in all of it even in the darkest and most painful of places.
You said the story isn't for me Jesus but I get to share in its treasure don't I?
Yes my little one you do. My gift to you is myself my little one and I am to be found everywhere and in everything. All you need do is learn how to find me.
And that is something you are wanting to teach me.
Yes my little one it is. It will help you to find hope even in the darkest of places my little one for I am always there in the midst.
You are going to have to help me a lot Jesus because when I think about all the evil things that happen in the world I don't see you. I see the enemy.
Yes my little one for that is what he wants you to see. He wants you to

look at him my little one for in that way he makes himself bigger in your eyes but I am far greater than he my little one. I am always there to be found.

Is it more deception?

Yes my little one everything he does is based on lies and deception. All of it is to draw you away from the truth.

The truth that you are in control and good.

Yes my little one. He would like you to believe that he is in control, that he is the one who decides what happens but it is not so my little one. I work through everything he does to bring my light into this world.

But people choose the darkness, they see it and believe in it.

Yes my little one they do. They are deceived in many ways my little one for darkness always seeks to obscure the light but it cannot do it my little one. The light is always there waiting to be revealed to those who will see it.

Can you give me an example Jesus, from my story maybe?

My little one when you look at your story what do you see?

Pain and cruelty and evil, I see the darkness Jesus, mostly anyway.

But I was always there with you my little one, the light never left you

But why do I see the darkness?

Pain and fear will always draw your attention to it my little one out learning to see the truth even in all of the pain and the cruelty, that is when you see the light that was present.

Ok, so I remembered you in some of the bad places Jesus. Like when I was hiding under the stairs and wanting to die and you were holding me. That was light in the darkness.

Yes my little one it was. My little one I have purpose in every part of your story.

So there is purpose in that part.

Yes my little one there is.

It helps me believe that you were always there with me even when I was looking at the darkness and couldn't see you. Is that it?

Yes my little one but there is more that you have not yet seen.

I am wondering what you were doing. I didn't know you were there but you were holding me. You were doing something.

Yes my little one I was.

What were you doing Jesus?

I was making you strong my little one, strong enough to endure through all of the darkness. The darkness did not overcome you my little one though it did everything it could to take your life from you it did not succeed.

Because you were there, the light overcame the darkness, even though, it seemed like there was no light.

Yes my little one. In every battle for your life I was there with you. I overcame everything that darkness did to you to enable you to survive my little one.

But what I see is what darkness did.

Yes my little one but learning to see what I did will help you to understand more of your story and more of who I am.

But when you say you overcame Jesus, I mean I suppose eventually you did but it is hard to see it in that moment.

That moment was intended to take your life my little one as were many others. The enemy was seeking to destroy you but he was not able my little one because I was with you.

I need to see it better Jesus. I need to see you better. And I am wondering about those who didn't survive. How does light, how do I see the light in those things?

I will show you my little one as you allow yourself to look at your story with eyes that are searching for the truth not just of what you saw and experienced but of who I am in those moments.

It sounds like a difficult thing Jesus but I see that it would be a good thing.

Yes my little one it will help you and through you many others.

Ok then. Help me look and help me see what I didn't before. Help me see you in everything.

Yes my little one I will.

> **I will smash down gates of bronze and cut through bars of iron. And I will give you treasures hidden in the darkness— secret riches. I will do this so you may know that I am the Lord, the God of Israel, the one who calls you by name. - Isaiah 45:2-3**

He watched over all of us together and separately knowing that the time would come when he would draw us close, heal us and teach us so many things about who he is, who we are, about the kingdom of God that we could only have learned by walking the path that he set before us. He sees the end from the beginning and that is why he allowed us to suffer, why he sent us back. Not alone, never alone but on a journey with him, for his sake and for the sake of those who are lost in the darkness just like we were.

You are loved my little one you are so loved. You are beautiful and special in every way to me. No matter what you do or what you say you

can never be more loved than you already are. You are my shining star. A treasure in the darkness my little one, a treasure that will be found by many as they seek healing. You are my promise to so many of my children my little one because of who you are in me.

The beatitudes make it clear that I am blessed. I am blessed even though I have been so hurt, even though I never received the things I needed as a child, even though I lost everything, even who I am. I am blessed because in my great need Jesus met me. He gave me what no person ever could. My need made me cling to him in all my pain and fear. It made me hold on to him because I had nowhere else to go. Only he knew how to meet my need, it wasn't overwhelming to him. The confusion I have felt about all the people who were meant to love me but instead hurt and betrayed me made me angry and suspicious and untrusting. He took all of that. He was never hurt or offended, never lashed out in return. Never lost patience or hope. Never failed to love me no matter what I said to him, no matter how I acted. No matter how many times I turned away or blamed him for the things people did. I have learned a lot about my Jesus because of my great need. I have learned to trust him when I am confused, and it seems like trusting him is the most stupid thing I could do. Like the beatitudes say I am blessed because I have received so much more than I lost. Far more than I would ever have been willing to receive if I hadn't been so empty, if I hadn't grown up never knowing what it was to feel safe and loved. Now I know it and it can never be taken away because it depends on him and on who he is and not on me or anyone else. I know who I am, not fully because I am still discovering it, but I know I am because he wants me to be. Not an accident, not unwanted but always loved, always safe.

"Blessed are the poor in spirit,
for theirs is the kingdom of heaven.
Blessed are those who mourn,
for they will be comforted.
Blessed are the meek,
for they will inherit the earth.
Blessed are those who hunger
and thirst for righteousness,
for they will be filled.
Blessed are the merciful,
for they will be shown mercy.

**Blessed are the pure in heart,
for they will see God.
Blessed are the peacemakers,
for they will be called children of God.
Blessed are those who are persecuted
because of righteousness,
for theirs is the kingdom of heaven.
Matthew 5:3-10**

Why did he want me to live knowing what I would suffer? Why didn't he let me die? Because his purpose for me remained the same. It didn't change because of what other people did to me. None of that changed who I am. None of that changed his love or his purpose or his plan for my life, all of which was hidden in my heart from the beginning. And even though my heart was broken and many of the seeds that were planted there were destroyed or uprooted he still saw me the same. He never gave up on me. He never saw me as beyond hope. He knew that he could take all of the things that have hurt me and use them for good. That the weeds, lies planted by the enemy, could be removed. That the soil could be made good again. That new seeds could be planted and those that had never grown could be brought back to life. He saw my heart as he had made it to be and he was glad he made it even after it had been trampled and disfigured. He saw me as worth saving, the person he made, whose birth he celebrated. He saw me the same in my broken crushed state as he did the first time, he thought of me and made me to be me.

He made me to be a light in the darkness, a light he rescued from the darkness. A light that would shine even brighter because of the things the darkness did. A light that the darkness couldn't destroy because he was always with me holding me close to his heart, keeping me safe even though I was hurt so much I should have died, should have been beyond saving. But nothing is too hard for him. No matter how lost I was, no matter how broken, I was worth saving. He celebrates my life. He celebrates me and nothing can or ever will change that.

Chapter 4

The Path to Wholeness

Our path before we met Jesus was a winding one. Even after some of the alters met and started to follow him it twisted and turned because choices were often made to turn away from him but he continued to draw us to him, one by one, until we were able to follow the path he had for us, to make the choice for ourselves.

Growing up in the middle of all that was happening meant living two lives. One life was filled with the horror of abuse, the cults, darkness, death and pain. The other life we were living was mostly very ordinary. We went to school, had friends, did all the normal things that children do. When we were eleven, we went to a new school and made new friends. This introduced us to our best childhood friend, Ellie. Ellie went to church and we started to go with her. Even then Jesus was working to draw us closer. It is strange to think it was the very same church where the priest who hurt us was the vicar, but he was gone now. I don't think he ever took us to that building so it didn't bother us to be there. Over the next few years that church became our second home and Ellie's family were the family we never had. She had a mum and a dad, sisters and cousins, aunts and uncles and a grandma. They all welcomed us and treated us with affection, as part of the family. It was a home from home, a safe place to be. Life at home with mum, even apart from the very bad things, wasn't happy. It wasn't filled with kindness, acceptance or love and encouragement. It was a place where we felt lonely, unhappy and often afraid. But Jesus gave us another home, another family who were a picture to me of how it could be. Not that they were perfect of course but there was love. Church had a youth group where we made friends, did fun things and even went away on holidays. We learned about Jesus and even though I'm not sure we really understood, we made a commitment. We knew there was something we needed.

Our other life in the cults took on a new horror as we got older, giving babies to the cult as sacrifices, taking part in the dismembering of victims, falling deeper into the darkness.

I remembered being stood in front of a flat stone. It was dark. I was wearing one of the red robes. Others had laid the body of a girl, maybe a teenager not a little girl, on the stone in front of me. I was the one who cut her open. I took out her intestines and her heart and gave them to children who took them away. It is very hard for me to believe these things are true. I saw me with a big knife like I had been taught how to use it and I cut through her neck, so her head came off and I did the same with her arms. The arms were taken away, but I pulled out one of her teeth and put it in a bowl with her blood. Maybe I ground it up I am not sure. Then I took it to the Goatman who was waiting in front of a crowd. It was a ceremony. The Goatman drank and then I did and then he did it to me on the stone alter. I was bare under my robe like he was. I seemed to be enjoying it. I knew that the reason for this was to make a baby. I don't understand it really. Then I remembered again, and I suppose this was months later because I was on the same stone and I had had a baby and the Goatman was holding it up. It still had the cord on and was kind of bloody. It was a little boy, he was very little. I was taken off the alter and the Goatman said some words and put down the baby on the stone. His name was Peter. I don't know who gave him that name. He put the knife Peter's heart. They didn't do bad things him like cut him up or put him on the fire. They made a little grave and laid him in it. He was special because he was my firstborn.

Maybe that darkness would have overtaken us, if it hadn't been for the love and light we found in our other life. Maybe the pain and despair and the shame would have overtaken us if I hadn't found some love and acceptance. When we were eighteen there was an evangelistic event in our neighborhood. I don't remember who they were or anything about them now, but they set up a big marquee and had meetings every night for two weeks. We went night after night. I don't remember anything that was said or anything that happened just the smell of the grass and the longing in my heart. I do know that I was different after that, that we had found something. Something had changed and we had a new understanding of who Jesus was and that he loved us. I am supposing now that some of the alters had met with Jesus, that the change happened on the inside as well as the outside.

It was a battle of course between the darkness and the light. One part of our life was totally given over to the darkness but now the light had claimed something back. The enemy was working to destroy us and through us to destroy others, but Jesus was working to bring us back into the light. To claim back what was lost and to make us completely his.

My dearest one I will show you how I see you story if you are willing.
Yes Jesus. I am willing. How do you see it?
Close your eyes my little one....
That is a very unexpected way to look at it Jesus.
Yes my little one but that is how I see it. Tell me what you saw.
I saw you, a bright light, you were all light and the darkness came and took a piece of light from you, from your heart Jesus. And the darkness took the little light away and hammered at it and screamed at it and froze it until the light was sealed in this dark ball, like when hot metal cools on the outside and makes a dark metal crust. But the light was still there on the inside but hidden away. And then you came and snatched away the dark metal ball from the darkness and you put it into your heart, just the way it was. And the dark crust melted away and the light joined with your light. It was beautful Jesus and it makes me want to cry but I never thought of it like that before.
But that is how it is my little one. You were taken from me and the darkness hurt you and tried to make you theirs but they could not do it my little one. Your light remained no matter what they did and you survived until I came and claimed you back for my very own. Darkness cannot survive in the light my little one. You are one with me again.

Of course, the only reason I was able to live this double life, to survive, was because of the alters. Some people think that DID is a mental illness but that isn't it at all. DID helped me to survive what should have killed me. It helped us to live a 'normal' life even when things were nowhere near normal. It enabled us to go to school, make friends, to laugh and to play and do all the things that 'normal' girls do with no one guessing the truth, not even the alters who were living the 'normal' life. Of course, many of the alters, including me, were depressed, suicidal, traumatized, but DID isn't itself an illness. It is a way to survive the un-survivable.

I haven't been able to fully work out who was who, who did what and when. It's very complicated with a lot of the alters sharing memories and experiences. Some only ever experienced trauma and pain and fear, others never knew those things happened at all. Jesus was in the midst with each one of us in the lives we lived separately and together. Only he could make sense of it. Only he could understand and know where each of us fitted into the whole. Only he knew what broke us and what would bring us back together. We didn't know. We only had pieces, each of us, like a jigsaw. I didn't see all of the pieces to the jigsaw until the healing was almost done. The picture took a long time to complete which I am glad of. It would have been too much to see it before most of it was healed.

Some alters belonged to Jesus all along. Some had given themselves to Satan, not freely but they were so lost in the darkness that it held on to them tightly. Jesus had to bring light and life to each of the alters but for now each one was living their own life. Some I can see when I remember things that happened but mostly its not clear. I do know that it wasn't me Pearl living that life. I was hidden away inside from the age of around three, kept safe from the things that were happening. Not able to live the normal life because of the hurt I'd already experienced. All the memories I have of the life that was lived from then until I gave myself to Jesus are the memories and experiences of other alters. Some I shared at the time, some later as Jesus was healing us but most of the life, I remember wasn't lived by me. Each alter is special and unique, created in love by Jesus. Each one helped us to survive what we couldn't have survived without each other.

On the outside life continued apparently normally. Leaving home was something we had looked forward to for a long time. We were desperate to leave. None of our friends were going to university, we were the only one. We were excited to go away and study, we enjoyed it, we were good at it and it was a way of escape. Our exam results were a disappointment though, maybe because we'd spent so much revision time at the tent meetings. Maybe because of the things that were happening in the cults, I'm not sure. It meant we had to choose a different university course to the one we'd planned but anything was better than staying where we were.

Even though we had been so desperate to leave we found it hard to settle and came home every weekend for the first year. Eventually though we settled in and lived the student life. On the outside all seemed well but under the surface there was always pain, fear and a desperate longing to be loved. We met the man we would marry. We were amazed anyone would love us and were determined not to end up alone, but we had no idea what love looked like. We ignored the warning signs. We got married aged twenty-two, but it was never happy. There were problems right from the start, but we couldn't turn back. When we thought we were pregnant it stirred up a desperate longing for a baby which I understand better now. It was a false alarm but now we decided to try for a child. It ended in a miscarriage, another lost child, though I didn't understand that then. No doubt there were some who did, and our grief was intense but there was no comfort. It was shrugged off by others as one of those things. The next pregnancy was complicated with a big scare at about four months and we were ordered to rest until the baby was born. But Sophie was born safe and healthy and we hoped that maybe things would improve. It seemed like it would at first. Our husband seemed pleased with his new daughter but after a while started to lose interest. It seemed like it was now or never, and the decision was made to have another child. We were tired and ill for most of the pregnancy, run down I suppose. Stressed and unhappy because now our husband had lost interest not just in Sophie but in the child that was coming. We were alone, no family, no friends in a new city with a husband who was really only interested in himself and his own needs.

I see now that it was our own desperate need to be loved and to have children to love when so many had been taken from us that led us down this path. I don't believe any of it was what Jesus had planned. When we first got to university, he sent people to our door from the Christian union, trying to draw us closer and lead us down a different path. But we turned away. The battle between the light and the darkness continued and for now the darkness had succeeded in drawing us into a life of loneliness, depression and despair.

After Richard was born, we sank lower, not coping, not sleeping, not really able to care for ourselves. Maybe another alter took over because we seemed to recover suddenly and started to meet other mums, taking the children out to groups. But Richard wasn't like other children. At age two he was diagnosed as autistic. It was devastating, like we lost another child. Our husband only seemed to grow angrier and more resentful of the children that took our time and energy. We began to understand that there was a choice to make. We had to protect Sophie and Richard. I don't know which alters took over, who had the strength and the will to leave but we did leave. When our husband broke contact we decided to move back home, back to the mother we had been so desperate to leave. Back to where we had come from. It is hard to escape from the past, to break free from the things that hold us.

My little one you are safe in my arms you are safe in our father's arms. That is where you are. Nothing and nobody can take you from us.
You've got to help me Jesus. You've got to help me...Crying.
I am here my little one I will help you.
I shouldn't be here, why am I still here. Why? I should have run and kept running and never come back. But instead I am still trapped here. I am still trapped just like I always was. After all of this time.

O my god why can't I get away. Why…Crying…Why?

Because my little one you are not ready to leave. My little one there have been many things that have kept you here, many reasons why you have not been able to leave. You are beginning to break free my little one, but it has taken time.

I can't be here I can't be here I can't. This is the wrong place for me. I shouldn't be here. I can't be here. I can't be here.

My little one hold on to me and listen to what I will say. I am setting you free my little one so that you are able to leave. I know my dearest one that everything within you is desperate to leave this place, but it would not be enough for you to leave this place physically my little one. There are many things which still hold you, things which would continue to hold you even if you were to leave. I would not have it so my little one. I want to set you free so that you can truly leave this place with all of its pain and never return my little one. That is what I want for you. I will make it possible my little one, but you need to hold on and trust me. I will not leave you here. I am doing a great work of healing my little one, one which is necessary so that you can truly leave this place. My little one I am enough for you. Hold on and do not let go. Remember all that I am to you and all that you are to me. I am healing you and setting you free my little one. I will not keep you here. This is not the life I have for you. I am setting you free so that you can go and do and be everything you were created for.

Help me.

I am here my little one I will not let you go.

I can't be here I can't be here.

Hold on my little one I will make it possible for you to leave. I love you my little one with all that I am, and I understand everything that is holding you in the place that you are in. I will not leave you here. I am working to set you free from everything that is holding you. Keep your eyes fixed on me my little one. I will not let you go.

I shouldn't be here.

No my little one you shouldn't. Hold on to me and let me set you free. Only I can do it my little one. You cannot free yourself. Hold on and trust me.

It was a new start in a town where I had good memories. Not the place we grew up but where our aunt, uncle and cousin lived and where we'd visited as a child. Mum had moved there when she retired with her husband, my stepdad.

I wasn't remembering the bad things yet. All of that was hidden away with the alters. Jennifer was the one on the outside most of the time I think, though sharing with others. It was better because mum and my aunt helped with the children. Jennifer started training to be a counsellor which seems strange now that I know about the past that was hidden away. She was good at it though and clever too. She studied up to master's level and worked with all kinds of people helping them to resolve issues, recover from abuse and live better lives.

This new direction was part of Jesus plan for us. Along the way Jennifer, and maybe others, started going to church, looking for the truth. She wanted to know if God was real and if he was whether it matters. Jesus had always been with us but now he started calling us closer. Jennifer made her decision for Jesus and a new part of our journey began. Jennifer wasn't interested in a going to church once a week Christianity. She knew that if Jesus is real then she wanted and needed to know him, she wanted to hear his voice. She wanted it to make a difference, she wasn't going to settle for religion.

Jesus had drawn us closer, all of us, through his relationship with Jennifer. We were on a path to healing and wholeness in Jesus, though we didn't know that yet. He was working through her choices to follow him on the outside and maybe through others on the inside to begin the long work of restoration. To make us whole and complete in Him.

Chapter 5

The Path of Preparation

Before Jesus could start healing us, he had to prepare us for what was coming. We didn't see it like that of course. We didn't know what was coming or what we would need. The first thing he taught us was to hear his voice clearly. Jennifer had been praying and asking ever since she met Jesus. She wanted to hear him. She didn't see why she shouldn't if all the things the bible said were true. That was the Holy Sprit drawing us closer, leading us down the path he had for us. But there was a battle right from the start. Just after Jennifer gave herself to Jesus the enemy came with their threats. We didn't know then of course that they had a hold on us, we didn't know anything. But they came in the night telling us they would never leave us alone, trying to make us afraid to follow Jesus.

The battle continued because the church we were in didn't believe in the things of the spirit. Dreams, visions, the gifts of the spirit, hearing God's voice directly, even talking to Jesus were all somehow 'wrong'. Jennifer refused to accept this and argued with the pastor about it. She kept seeking and Jesus made a way. Soon she was baptized in the spirit, speaking in tongues, having dreams and visions and hearing Jesus speak directly to her. She followed him and he gave her the desires of her heart, desires he gave her of course. We moved to a new church where we were encouraged to grow and learn. This was the first thing we needed. Now we could hear him and accept the things of the spirit as real and true and Jesus started to talk about his plans for us. They seemed far off and exciting, they seemed impossible. But he spoke directly, he spoke through dreams and visions and through other people. Always saying the same thing, that he had a ministry for us to bring healing and hope.

February 2007 (Hazel Carr)

God is pulling you towards Himself, separating you out for Himself. He is going to use you, you will be a tool in his hands to speak truth and bring freedom to people. This is for the future. He's doing a work now, He's going to use everything you have gone through, all the circumstances of your life and He's going to use them to make you into someone He can use. He's doing something in you, making you beautiful.

You have a warm heart. You will receive revelation and you will know you have heard God's voice. You will have the Lord's compassion for those you minister to. You will experience opposition from people but the Lord will be with you and He will bring them to a place of softness and compassion. God is raising you up. He is doing beautiful things in your life. You will speak forth the word of God, bringing truth. You'll speak with authority. You are being called to a position at leadership level in the future. There is a tremendous anointing upon you.

Even though we knew that counselling was part of the path Jesus had for us he began to show us that there was something more he had for us. That what he wanted to do through us wouldn't come through working as a counsellor. It was time for a new thing.

I went on a retreat day with the people I worked with. It was supposed to be a day to spend with God but it turned out to be a lot of boring talking. At the lunch break I got overwhelmed by a desperate need to go to the little chapel I had seen when I arrived. It was so strong I had to go even though the people I was with thought I was very rude I think. When I got there I sat for a little while and I heard Jesus say so very clearly in my heart 'I have not called you to this'. He said it three times so there was no mistake. I sat there not really knowing what to do. I saw a little alcove with some candles in it. It looked nice, hidden away and there was a little seat so I went and sat and looked at the tiny tea light candles that were there and I heard him again. 'I have not called you to this, this is tea-light ministry, a little light, a little power....' I looked up and saw a skylight in the ceiling and he said 'the ministry I will give you will be as the sun compared to this. You will open up the windows of heaven and let the sunshine down on the people. Your ministry will be like the sun compared to the tea-light'. I was so shocked. I sat there with my mouth open for ages.

That wasn't all though. A few days later I went to a meeting where there was worship and a speaker. Most of it was very boring but then one of the speakers said that the Holy Spirit was calling people to go forward and make a fresh commitment. It was like there was fire in my heart and I practically ran to the front and fell on my knees. It was complete surrender to whatever Jesus was asking. It was a kind of scary no turning back moment but I couldn't help it. I was crying and crying and shaking all over. I heard a click like something had clicked into place and I saw the word 'commissioned' written in little golden letters over me. Later on, while I was lying awake that night, Jesus showed me what the click was. He showed me a picture of railway points...they had shifted and clicked into place so that now my life was on a different track.

We didn't understand a lot of it, but it was clear he was leading us somewhere. He gave us hope and a purpose. That was the second thing we needed.

Now he began to show us our need for healing. He went slowly at first only showing us things we knew but hadn't really seen for what they were. He began speaking to us about the healing he wanted to do, leading us step by step, building trust and confidence in what he was doing. We understood for him to work through us, to fulfil the promises he had made to us, he first had to work in us and heal us. His promises gave us a reason to follow him into healing. They gave purpose to it. That was the next thing we needed, to choose healing. He showed us as much as he could what it was going to mean so that we could choose his path. We couldn't know of course what it would really mean for us, but we knew enough to make a choice.

I saw the Lord coming towards me, across a floor of what looked like thousands of gemstones. His feet were at my eye- level and I couldn't see where I was, I couldn't see myself. Jesus squatted down and held out His hand towards me and pulled me out of a pit? I didn't see it but I was covered in black goo. As we walked back across the gems I could see I was leaving a trail of black goo across them. We then came to a perfectly white environment and then I saw myself. I was filthy, ragged with matted black long hair which trailed on the floor behind me. I was disgusting. The Lord continued to almost pull me along as I grew more and more distressed at my state and the mess I was leaving in my wake. I tried to stop, I tried to let go of Him but He kept a firm hold and urged me onwards. We came to a door which Jesus opened. Inside was a storm? Crashing waves, gale force wind, driving rain and in amongst it all fire. Jesus motioned for me to go in. I knew this was where I would be cleansed but I was afraid- it was terrifying in there. As I stepped into the room Jesus came with me. As I was engulfed by the storm I was aware of Him holding me and that is what I focused on. Finally Jesus led me out of the room by a different door. Outside it was still and completely white again. I stood before Him, bedraggled and battered, in

41

my rags. I looked at Jesus.. He was in the same condition. He had experienced every blow and every pain that I had. He had truly been with me. As I looked at Him a great blinding light shone on us. It was warm and gentle. We were warmed, dried and healed. Jesus exchanged my rags for a white gown which sparkled. My hair was now shoulder length, golden in color. Jesus put a netting of golden gems onto my head, he took my hand and we walked across the floor again. This time I left a trail of crystal-clear footprints. Jesus led me to the floor of gems. This time as I walked across them what had been dull jewels now sparkled and gleamed.

When we were ready he chose the perfect time and place to begin his work. He gave us a dream which told us he was going to break down the barriers in our mind, that he would do it at an event we were going to. We didn't understand at the time of course but later it made sense, later it helped us to trust in what he was doing. We went to the conference prepared for something to happen but not knowing what it was. The first thing he did was to give us a word of encouragement from the minister who was preaching, that I am called to be an evangelist. We found that confusing because it wasn't what were expecting, or even wanting but I understand now that it was a kind of strength he was giving us, speaking our purpose over us before he began. The Holy Spirit was so tangible in that meeting there was no question that he was at work. The opposition of the enemy to what was happening was so obvious that it just confirmed it. And what happened was such a turning point that we knew had to be God and it helped us trust what followed. Something that we needed when everything we thought we knew was uncertain.

We arrived in time for the evening meeting. Ruth wanted to sit right at the front. She knew the woman who was speaking so maybe that is why but I wanted to hide at the back. I was feeling very scared. I was scared that Jesus was going to do something and I was scared that he wasn't. I'm not sure how much I managed to worship or pay attention to the message but I did pay attention when the lady speaker stopped in the middle of her sermon and pointed straight at me. I was right in front of her of course. She said to me you are called to be an evangelist, you don't know it but you are. Maybe I looked as shocked as I felt I don't know. I just sat there. I think I felt sick and very, very confused. This was not what I had been expecting at all. Why was he doing this? How was it meant to help? I didn't want to be an evangelist. I thought it was stupid but I couldn't argue with it. That lady was very, very certain about what she was saying.

The lady continued with her message but I wasn't listening. I was having a little rant at Jesus. Meanwhile the lady stopped preaching because the presence of the Holy Spirit was so strong she couldn't even stand. She called people to come forward for prayer and even though I was confused about what had happened I knew I had to go. But I was overwhelmed by a terrible fear and a despair that said to go forward was a waste of time, that nothing was going to happen. Jesus wasn't going to do anything. I struggled and wrestled for a while. I knew I had to go even if I thought it was a waste of time. At least that way I was letting Jesus decide what to do and not getting in the way of that. But even so it was like I was glued to the seat. A lady came and sat next to me. She said she could see I was afraid but felt I really needed to go forward. I started to cry and said yes but I couldn't. I prayed and I prayed and I suppose that Jesus helped me because I found myself on my feet walking to the front. I know now that it was the enemy trying to keep me from what Jesus was about to do but right then all I felt was fear and confusion.

I joined the end of the row of people who were waiting for the lady to pray for them. She had got back on her feet by now but she never prayed for me. The Holy Spirit just came and I fell to my knees crying and crying. There was so much pain that came from somewhere deep, deep inside. I didn't know what it was or what was happening but I knew it was the Holy Spirit at work. I knew this was what I had come for. I cried and cried and cried. I made a lot of noise. I am glad it was a noisy room full of people but even so I made a lot of horrible wailing noises. I couldn't stop it. It just kept coming and coming. People came and gave me words like that I would do great things for God because I had surrendered and that he was giving me a testimony. That was nice but what I really wanted was someone to give me a lot of tissues because I was very much needing them!

When I asked Jesus later about being an evangelist he said you have no idea who you are. You are who I say that you are. That is something he has said a lot to me as I have been learning about who I am. Learning that he sees the truth about who I am and accepting that has been so important.

**You are not who you think you are, not in any sense but I will
give you a new identity, a new name. This is what I will do. I
make all things new. Do not be afraid. I am holding you. I will
give you the strength to see the truth, trust me to do that. There
is nothing to know that you cannot bear. You are strong in me
my little one, so strong. Nothing can stop this now. I will
completely heal and cleanse you. It will not be long now. Just
hold on to me and know that I am all you need. I will show you
the truth and I will bring you out of that into a future full of life
and freedom. Take it one step at a time, just follow me. Don't
worry about the path and where it leads.**

He had prepared us well and now Jesus began to reveal the
truth of the bad things to us. That was so hard to accept, that those
things could have happened, and we had somehow forgotten it. But
because we trusted Jesus enough, and because we had chosen to
follow him, he was able to lead us forward. Now we were ready for
the truth, the truth of the bad things and the truth of the alters. Jesus
had prepared us for it step by step. We saw that even then and it
helped us to accept the new memories and alters even though it
seemed more than we could bear. He had told us in many ways,
even before we saw it, that there were many of us.

*I saw a flower, a bit like a chrysanthemum. At first it was
white, then yellow, then pink. Then there was a bunch of
them. The Lord picked one out and gave it to me. It was
white with a red center. Then He gave me a yellow one, then
pink, all with red centers. He said you are not one thing but
many. I saw a diamond but it was full of many colors. Again I
felt the Lord was saying not one but many.*

He had spent time talking to us about the healing that needed
to be done. He had helped us to trust him and to choose his way. He
gave us a point in time to look at knowing that was when the walls
came down. Understanding it was his work to heal us did make a
huge difference.

**I will reclaim you and restore you my child. There is none that
can stop me. I will have my way. You must find all of your
strength in me, all of it. Do not rely on your own strength for
anything. Lean on me in all things. I am sufficient. I will supply
every need you have. I will make you whole again my beloved
child. Only I know the way, the way I have chosen for you. Do**

not lean on your understanding but only on mine. I will not let you falter or fall. I am with you. I am with you. Remember these words. I am with you. I never leave you. I never forsake you. I am working for you. I am fighting for you. I am your protector and your healer. I will save and deliver you from all the woks of the devil. Place yourself completely in my hands. You cannot do this. You cannot do this. I am completely trustworthy. I will not let you down. I will not hurt you. I will not give you more than you can bear.

"He who has an ear, let him hear what
the Spirit has to say to the churches.
To him who overcomes, I will give
some of the hidden manna. I will
also give him a white stone
with a new name written on it,
Known only to him who receives it."

Revelation 2:17

Chapter 6

The Path of Healing

Jesus had prepared us, but healing didn't come straight away. That was confusing to us. It didn't come the way we expected either or through people we thought would help us and be there for us. We had to hold on to Jesus and trust that he would make a way for us. Knowing that this was his plan and his work helped a lot with that even though it was far from easy. We thought at first that our help would come from the ministry center Jesus had sent us to. We went there believing we were learning how to minister but now we were the ones in need. But they couldn't help, too needy, too time consuming, not the words they used but that's the way it was. We asked our pastor who promised to help or to find help, but no help came. We searched the internet but there was no help that was close enough or that we could afford or felt we could trust. The counsellor Jennifer had worked for agreed to help but she was overwhelmed I think, and it was no help to us. We didn't want to go to mental health services because we didn't trust them having seen what Jennifer's clients in the system often went through and more than that we knew Jesus had to be at the center of the healing. This was his plan and his work.

Then out of the blue we went to the revival that was going on in Florida. We found that the church at the center of what was happening had a ministry to people with DID and we knew it wasn't a coincidence. Even though there was no long term help we came back knowing that Jesus was still with us, still working to bring us hope and healing even if we couldn't see how yet.

The lack of help from everyone we turned to made us desperate, desperate enough to look in places we wouldn't otherwise have looked. That is how he led us to daddy Mike through his books. We didn't know how much help he could be when he was in a different country but at least we knew he understood more than we did about the bad things, about what was happening. And most importantly he knew Jesus and he agreed to help us. I see now that Jesus was directing our path to the place he wanted us to go.

The battle grew fiercer. The enemy tried everything to convince us we couldn't trust daddy Mike, that he wouldn't help, that there was no hope. We didn't understand why Jesus had led us to him most of the time to begin with.

Lord why must it be this way, isn't there enough going on for me?

My child I ask you to trust me. Things are not always what they seem.

I don't understand how a man who does not have time and does not care can help me in any way at all.

You must trust me to work through all this. I know Mike's heart and you do not, it is all in the palm of my hand. Do not doubt me.

I don't like it. How can I stop it from hurting?

By holding on to me. I will help you bear the pain.

But why must I bear this extra pain. Don't I have enough already?

Remember that I am working all things for your good. All things, even this.

Yes I remember but I'm not sure that I can keep going Lord, how can I write so personally to this man?

Think of it as writing to me, know that I am listening and I am responding, whether you see it or not. Know that whether you are aware of it or not Mike is listening. He is paying attention. He is bringing all of you before me. He does care.

But Jesus had more and bigger plans than we knew. He had plans for us to be partners in ministry, for him to be my daddy. Helping us heal was only the beginning.

You are my Pearl and as you go through this life loving and serving me you will do so side by side with my servant. He is given to you to love you and teach you and guide you as a father would. That is who he is to you my little one. That is your need.

Even though we grew to trust him and love him, and he helped us in many ways Jesus never let us depend on Daddy Mike. We learned to turn to Jesus first, in everything, to trust him over and above anyone or anything that we thought we needed. That was so hard when we were so desperate and felt so alone but that was his path for us. He didn't want me to be dependent on Daddy Mike for my faith or my healing but only on him. So, Daddy Mike was a friend and an encourager and helped us a lot in understanding and to keep going, but he was never involved in any of the healing that Jesus did, not in any of the rescues or battles with the enemy. He prayed for us I know but hardly ever with us. There was never any doubt who was in control, who was healing us, leading us and whose plan we were following.

Jesus chose to heal us directly, not through any other person. He had prepared us for this by giving us the ability to hear him clearly and to trust him. He healed us through relationship with him, with the Holy Spirit and daddy God, often separately sometimes together. My healing path has helped me to understand many things about Jesus the Holy Spirit and daddy God. It has drawn me closer to all of them and it began with Jennifer.

Jesus began with Jennifer, healing her so that she would be strong enough for what was ahead. She had to be so strong in Jesus to keep the outside life going, managing to do all the things she needed to in caring for two teenagers and a house whilst on the inside everything was falling apart. There was pain and fear and alters surfacing with memories that were too horrific to believe. She held it together through all of that because Jesus gave her the strength she needed. We all learned through this that Jesus is our strength and can enable us to do the seemingly impossible. Something he has continued to teach us all the way along our path with him.

Jesus was in front of me squatting down and I was sitting in the dirt like the day before. Then I need more of you Jesus and the Holy Spirit and daddy. You've got to help me because I can't even get up......Crying.

Do you want to come with me my little one into all that I have promised you? Will you take my hand and continue to walk with me no matter what the cost. No matter how hard and how endless it seems?

Because that is the choice?

Yes my little one it is but it is not a hopeless one. It is a choice which will lead you to life my little one. My life and all that I am.

It is about choosing you.

Yes my little one it is. Always.

I do choose you Jesus I do but I can't do it......Crying

Not in your own strength my little one but you are not alone. I will help you and lead you and guide you and give you all that you need. You can walk this path with me my little one. It was made especially for you and you walk it with me in my strength.

I see that Jesus.

I know you do my little one. Come then take my hand and let me take you forward into all that I have for you. Trust me my little one. I am for you in every way.

So I held out my hand and he picked me up in his arms and I buried my face in his chest and cried.

He has taught us through all the hard choices we have needed to make how to trust him to give us the strength we needed, for everything he asked of us. Jesus took Jennifer through memories, directly into the pain and the fear. She trusted him enough to go where he wanted to take her.

I went into the kitchen and mum was there, doing something but with her back to me, ignoring me. I went into the little room under the stairs. The only thing I remember about this room was that was where we kept the record player, one of the old one with the lids. I loved the record player, it was a treat to be allowed to put the records on. But anyway this had nothing to do with that. I put myself right in the darkest corner under the stairs, there was no natural light in this room so it was dark and tried to make myself so small that I would disappear. I didn't want to exist. I didn't so much cry as howl with the pain of this memory. Jesus was there reassuring me, comforting me. And then I saw Him in the memory, holding me in His arms. I wasn't alone. He was there with me.

We all learned that we could trust him with our pain, that he knew how much we could bear and just what we needed. We learned that his comfort and his healing were enough for us no matter how deep the pain and the fear went.

My little one I am here. Do not be afraid but come to me with everything. My dearest one I am here with you. I will strengthen you and sustain you through everything my dearest one.
I'm sorry I just don't want to do this anymore. I don't want to face it. I don't want it to be real…crying.
My little one I am here with you. There is nothing you cannot do with me helping you. My dearest one I understand your pain and your fear but all you must do is hold on to me and follow me step by step. Do not worry about what lies ahead but concentrate on what I am giving you today. My little one that is enough. I am here with you. Hold on to me and all that I am. My little one the healing I have for you will come slowly that is true, for it is all that you can bear, but it will come my little one. Do not be afraid of what lies ahead but follow me. I know the perfect way for you. I will not lead you anywhere you cannot go.
I know but help me because I don't want to do it anymore. I don't I'm sorry. Please don't make me talk about it please...Crying.
My little one I will only go at the pace you can manage. I am not asking anything of you that you cannot do in my strength. My little one I know you are afraid but do not let that fear keep you from stepping into all that I have for you. My little one there is life before you, even in the

midst of all the pain. My little one I would not ask it of you if it were not so. Do not be afraid of anything I will ask of you for it is all working for you my little one. My way is perfect for you. Keep walking then and do not be afraid.

He wasn't just teaching us this for our sake but for the sake of those he has plans for me to reach. He wants me to give away everything I've received on the path so that others can walk their own paths towards everything Jesus has for them.

I am tired but I'd like to try and understand what you're doing if that's ok.

I want you to understand as much as you can my child and not merely for your sake but for others who will come after you.

What do you mean?

There are many others my child, who also require my healing.

Yes, I know.

I do not want them to be afraid. I want you to help them not to be afraid of the pain that comes with healing.

Who are these people and how can I help them?

You can help them because you have experienced the power of my healing love for yourself my child. There will be many people that I bring to you, many people who are afraid to surrender themselves and trust me with their pain as you have done. You will help them to trust me my dearest child because you will know and understand that no matter how terrible the pain, that I am there with you in it enabling you to bear it and loving you through it.

We didn't realize it at first, but Jesus wasn't only healing her but those of us hidden away on the inside. Some of the people he wanted to reach, that were afraid to trust him with their pain, were the alters like me, who were hidden away, but seeing and experiencing Jesus through her. We weren't strong enough to receive his healing directly, we didn't even know we existed but through Jennifer he was able to bring us enough healing so that we could begin to see who we were and come to Jesus for ourselves.

My little one even though Jennifer was the one on the outside, the one who was seen and known you were not hidden from me. You were always the one that I was healing my little one. Jennifer was strong enough to carry you through for me, so that I could begin healing you and separating you from her. I know my little one that this does not seem fair to you that I should have asked her to carry so much but that was my purpose for her my little one. She bore her burden well and did not regret anything that I asked of her.

So all those times Jennifer spent in your arms being healed, it was me that you were healing and not her.

You were the one that was hurting my little one. I brought healing to Jennifer in all the ways that she needed but the healing of the past was for you my little one and though it seemed to you both that I was healing her my healing was being given through her to you.

Why did she have to go through all that pain Jesus?

Because you needed her to be there my little one. You were not strong enough on your own.

Like scaffolding?

Yes my little one like a support that enabled you to receive my love and my healing. My dearest one the things that hurt you left wounds so deep that if I had separated you before bringing a measure of healing you would not have survived.

But I suppose I thought I didn't get hurt so much because Jennifer, others maybe like Aj, were like a shield.

No my little one that is only true in part. The alters that surrounded you and kept you safe were entwined within you, supporting you and giving you enough strength to survive. There was shielding my little one that came from being inside, hidden away, but the alters themselves were like an internal support. Without them you would not have lived my little one even hidden away as you were.

So they were a bit like life support?

Yes my little one.

And you healed me through them so that you could slowly take them away and I could be without them and not die.

Yes my little one that is so.

That is a bit different to what I thought.

It is not so different my little one. They helped you to survive. That was their purpose my little one.

As alters began coming to the surface they would talk with Jennifer, learning about Jesus from her. We learned at the same time of course. Jesus was reaching out to so many of us through her. I think it helped Jennifer too, to see the part she had to play, even though it meant she experienced the pain and the fear of those hidden away inside and had to endure the insults and taunts of some of the alters, who didn't think much of Jesus and his plans for us.

You are such a sad bitch get a life why don't you.

51

I've got one thanks.

Yeah well you ought to try living it a bit more, you and your saddo friends talking about Jesus this and Jesus that, you make me sick, like he ever did anything. What the hell is wrong with you? Just get on with life and leave him out of it.

So that's the problem, you're pissed off because I'm following Jesus and doing what he wants and not what you want.

So what if I am. My god you think you've got it sorted. Like he's going to come through and make it all better- give me a break! Why do you think we are in this mess in the first place? I'll tell you why because this Jesus, this God of yours doesn't give a shit. He let those bastards do unspeakable things to us, to all of us and to other kids too and did he do anything? He did not he just stood there and watched. I saw him. He didn't think so but I did. I was watching all the time and I saw Jesus standing there just watching it all happen. Well if he's God-all-fucking- mighty and he cares so much he could have stopped those bastards, but no he just stood there and watched so when I see you doing what he wants and going on about how wonderful he is, it makes me sick to my stomach you got me, it makes me want to rip you apart, because you're so sad and pathetic. He's the one you ought to be angry with, he's the one you ought to hate but not you, no you don't get angry do you? You just forgive them and have compassion and all that fucking shit. I don't believe you. Even your mum, shit that woman left us, she left you. She walked away, time after time she walked away. I saw it, I saw it all. I can't believe you can even look at the bitch, she left us for god's sake. She didn't care, none of them cared! Stop looking for someone to care nobody ever will! This is a shitty world from beginning to end, why don't you see that you stupid idiot. I can't stand it anymore you hear me, I can't stand it! I've got so much anger I could just, ahhhh I can't even say it and what's the point, you don't listen, you never listen, you tell me to shut up all the time and I just want you to see. I just want you to stop being a fucking doormat because they don't care got it! I don't care who it is, they only care about themselves. You are so stupid! What are you doing? You should know better than to trust people never mind God. I watch you, you think I'm not there but I watch you and just want to shout but you don't listen and you don't let me out and they are going to hurt you, hurt us all over again and I can't stand to watch it, I can't, don't make me watch it, please just stop ok.

Matilda we are all in so much pain. I cry and you shout, that's how we react. I don't know how to get through this and I'm sorry you had to watch and experience all that stuff. I'm sorry you've been hurting all this time. I don't want to fight with you. We are on the same side. I know you think I'm wrong. I can see why, can I make a suggestion?

What?

Why don't you talk to Jesus himself, tell him what you told me, see what he says.

Fuck, why?

Well why not, maybe it would help you to tell him how you feel.

Sure like he's going to listen to me. It's not like he cares.

Well what have you got to lose?

Fine. I bump into him I'll tell him what I think.

You don't have to wait. Why don't I ask him to come and be with us now?

Shit I don't want to talk to him.

Matilda this has been going on too long. It's time for things to change. Tell him how you feel.

Shit you tell him your so buddy, buddy, with him.

I could but how would that help? You need to talk to him not me.

Fine go on then. Tell him to come.

Jesus. My Jesus please come and talk to us.

I am here my child. I have been here all along. I have heard your cries Matilda. I was not deaf as you suppose but you were not ready to listen to my answer.

Fine so what is your answer? How could you stand there and let them do that to us. You are supposed to be full of love. What shit is that? Go on you tell me.

Matilda it was never my will that any of you should be hurt. I did not desire that. I do not desire pain and cruelty. But my love has given free

53

will to all people, including you, to choose your own way in this life. The people that hurt you chose evil and they inflicted great pain and suffering on you all. I was with you as you saw. I have always been with you. I have never left you not even for a moment though you did not always see me. I allowed you to see me in those moments so that now I could show you my heart and who I truly am. Are you ready to listen Matilda? For I cannot make you listen. I can speak the truth but you must be ready to accept it.

Go on then.

I was with you all along Matilda. I was with you all, for you are my children. I have been watching over you and caring for you though you have not perceived it. I saw and experienced all that was done, just as you did Matilda. I was the one who gave you all the strength and the ability to survive such cruelty and hate. I am the one who has brought you to this point so that you can now begin to choose which path you will take. Will you choose anger and hatred Matilda, or will you chose truth and life as I enable you. I give you that choice just as I gave it to them. Will you make a better choice than they did?

Shit, I don't know what you are talking about. Those evil bastards made choices to do things I would never do. Don't you compare me to them.

They chose to hurt and destroy Matilda... their methods may have been more extreme but was their choice any different?

You saying I'm choosing to hurt and destroy?!

Yes I am.

Shit!

My child what do you see?

Me lord?

Yes my dearest child.

That's a hard question because I get confused and I am full of pain. But Matilda is really just the same, confused and full of pain. We all are. How could we not be? I see that you love us though I don't always understand how you can allow such terrible things to happen to those you love, I don't know if I ever will. But you do love us and I don't want to choose to hurt and destroy. I don't think Matilda wants to choose that either.

What do you think about that Matilda? This child of mine has been hurt just as you have and yet she chooses my way.

Yeah well she didn't see did she. She shut her eyes and turned away. That was her choice.

Perhaps, but now she has seen and she is making her choice in spite

of that. **Come Matilda you know I speak the truth. You know the truth when you hear it for you have always valued the truth have you not?**

Yes, I suppose, I don't know, how am I supposed to understand you?

Will you accept me though you don't understand me?

What do you mean accept you?

Accept the truth as I reveal it to you my dearest child. That I am the one who loves you, that I have always loved you and although terrible things have happened to you I never forsook you and I never will. I can help you find life Matilda? Will you accept it? Will you accept me?

Shit I don't know. You are confusing me. I'm supposed to be angry with you.

You use your anger as a shield Matilda, to keep all the pain you feel from really touching you. But that anger will destroy you and those around you. Will you let it go and feel the pain? Will you choose better than they did?

Stop it. I'm not like them, I don't want to be like them but I don't know how to stop being angry I just am.

Let me help you Matilda. Give me the burden you carry and I will give you mine. My burden is light but yours is heavy.

I don't know. I'm tired of all this, let me think about it ok. I can do that right?

Yes. Consider well Matilda. Choose life in me or continue to choose death my child. For that is always the choice.

I don't want to choose death. We've had enough of that. I don't know who you are. I'm confused. Leave me alone for a bit ok.

Call me Matilda when you want to speak again. I will be there.

Fine ok.

My child.

Yes Jesus.

Do not be distressed my child. I am at work in ways that you cannot see. There is much to be done my dearest child but it is I who will do this. Rest in my love.

I will try, please be with me.

I am with you my child.

I know but I need so much more, I'm sorry.

It is my delight to meet your need my dearest child. Do not be afraid.

As we grew stronger Jesus began to separate those alters, we called the dollies. That was Aj, Blossum, dolly4 and dolly5. We called them the dollies because Jesus said they were like Russian dolls or paper dollies all folded together and hidden behind each other. It took time to separate them out so that he could heal each one separately.

Eventually Aj was strong enough to start taking over from Jennifer on the outside. Jesus told her that she was going to be the one on the outside, that she would be blended with Jennifer. We didn't understand this, it made no sense to us.

My little one everything that I have for you is good, everything that I ask of you is for your good. Do not be afraid my little one. I will hold you and protect you and enable you to be and do all that you need to be and do my little one. The only difference is that you will be relying upon me and not upon Jennifer.
So you will do what she does?
I will do it better my little one there is nothing to fear.
But I don't want them to see me Jesus. Even if I can do everything I need to I don't want them to see me.
My little one you are hidden in me there is nothing to fear. I will keep you safe. I will keep you protected and secure. No one will see you that you do not want to see you my little one.
That would be no one then. I don't understand. Is it just about dependence?
It is about dependence and trust my little one. This will require you to trust me and to depend upon me for everything.
I don't think I like it.
I know my little one but I will show you that I am safe and that I will keep you and give you all that you need.
It doesn't seem like something I can do.
I know my little one but you can do everything that I ask of you. I will enable you.
I don't like it.
My little one everything I am has been given to you, you belong to me, every part of you belongs to me. I love you with an everlasting love, I will not ever let you go or fail you in any way. You are safe in my hands my little one, no matter what I ask of you.
I know that must be true but I don't feel safe.
But you will my little one, as you surrender yourself more completely into my hands you will feel more safe than you have ever done. My little one my way for you is good, do not fear it.
I will try.
I will be enough for you my little one.

Over time Aj grew stronger and more able and she was the main alter on the outside for about two years, something we never thought would be possible. But Jesus made it possible. We learned even more about trusting and depending on Jesus through this and again when Blossum took over. Blossum was even younger than Aj, Aj was sixteen Blossum only eleven but that wasn't the end. Blossum was on the outside for two years and then Jesus drew me out, Pearl Sunshine, only nine years old. It made no sense to us, but we knew that it didn't matter really if I was only nine because everything I needed would come from Jesus. We didn't know at first of course just how much he would ask of me.

For years Jennifer had been the main outside alter. To begin with I think we all believed she was at the center and that all the alters probably came from her and would eventually be blended back with her. If our help had come from any of the other places we had tried and who said no, I don't think they would have accepted Jesus plan to have me on the outside, to be the one everyone else blended into. The ministry center we asked for help didn't even believe a woman could have male alters, I doubt they would have seen having a child alter as the one everyone else was blended with as possible or desirable or even as healing. Nor do I think many other counsellors or ministers would have been able to accept it. Daddy Mike was different because he listened to and trusted Jesus. He followed even though the path was strange and not what our ideas of healing would look like. Jesus plan didn't make much sense, definitely not to us. There were a lot of alters, a lot of adults who would have seemed a better choice, most especially to me.

My little one when I made you to be you I made someone who is precious and beautiful. I made someone so very special my little one someone with the capacity to do and be so many things that an adult does, but who is a child and sees and understands as a child does. My little one I will ask many things of you that a child could never do but that does not matter my little one because I am the one who will help you to do them. The things you do may be many of the things I would ask an adult to do but that does not take away anything that you are my little one. You do everything in my strength and not in your own. That means that you are capable of many things that a child would not ordinarily be capable of but that does not mean that you are not a child my little one.

But why did you make me a child if I can never be one?

My little one you will always be a child. You see and understand as a

57

child does but with a wisdom that comes from me and a life that has taught you many things. My little one the life I have for you will require you to draw upon all of these things. You are a child my little one because that is what I want you to be. It will be an asset my little one and not a hindrance in all that I ask you to do. My little one I know that you fear you will never be able to be the child that you are, to have the things that a child does. The love and care of people who will be there for you, a home where you will belong, acceptance. I know that you long to be able to run and play and to do and experience all the things that a child would as a child my little one. I know everything that is in your heart my little one. There is no part of you that I do not treasure. You have been in the garden many times my little one and you have seen how it is growing and becoming more and more full of life. My little one there is not any part of that garden that will be left untended, no secret places that will not be unlocked and brought back to life. Every part of you is precious to me my little one.

That's what I don't understand. It's like the child part of me has to be pushed away and ignored. Just like it always was. And if you don't want that, if there is no place for it why be cruel. Why not make me grown up or put a grown up in my place. I don't understand …Crying

My little one there is no one who can ever take your place. You are you my little one and every part of you is precious to me. I know it is hard for you to understand my little one but all the things I have said to you are true. Whilst you are here I have been helping you to grow strong in me and to trust and understand that you can do all things in my strength no matter what I will ask of you. I have asked you to live as an adult even though you are a child my little one so that you could learn these things. That does not mean my little one that I have forgotten who you are or the things that you need only that I am helping you to grow strong in this place so that when the time is right you are able to go forward into the life that I have prepared for you. There you will be able to grow in other ways my little one and to be the child that you are even whilst you are continuing to live in my strength doing all the things that I will ask of you.

Jesus took us on a journey of healing that we could never have expected. If he had told us everything he had planned from the beginning and what it would mean I don't think we would have followed him, but he gave us just enough and led us step by step along the path he chose. He took us from being a strong intelligent mature woman to being a child of nine, hidden in an adult's body with not much to offer except a willingness to follow and a trust and dependence entirely on Jesus. It always reminded me of Gideon's army (Judges 6). It still does.

Jesus plan was always for me, Pearl, to be on the outside. To be the one that everyone else blended with. He led us step by step down the path of healing he had for us. The path of healing he took us on taught us to trust him completely not only with the past and all of its pain but with the present and the future. We learned to depend on him for everything knowing that we, and especially me as a child, could never do the things that were being asked of me without his help. I learned that anything is possible with him because he led me down a path that meant I was living an impossible life even before I reached the City of Hope and his promises.

Chapter 7

Healing from the Inside Out

Jesus has healed all of us together and separately by taking us back into memories, back into the darkness of what happened to us and bringing his light and love and comfort to those places, but he has healed us in other ways too. He began by taking Jennifer onto the attic, a place in the spirit that was filled with boxes. Each of the boxes contained feelings and memories that had been hidden away. We opened the boxes one by one. It was a way for us to understand what had happened and it meant we could make the choice the open the box or not. It also meant that we didn't get overwhelmed and learned to take our healing one box at a time. It was a way of helping us heal but also of teaching us spiritual truths at the same time.

My child do remember what I did a little while ago, I unblocked the pathways in your mind and opened many doors that had been shut for so long?
Yes I remember.
There is a room that we must enter now. Will you come with me into this room?
Yes I will come. Help me because I am afraid.
I am with you my child. I am holding your hand. Do not be afraid.
Ok.
Tell me what you see.
It's like an old attic room, dark and dusty. Looks quite empty
Look again.
There are many boxes stacked up neatly against the walls, actually I'm thinking huddled so as not to be noticed.
What else to you see?
Another door at the far end of the room. It's shut...
So we walked over to the door and Jesus opened it. It was like opening into space, black, empty.
Speak my child.
Ok. What is that?
That is your fear my child, or at least how you see it, unending, bottomless. You keep the door shut but see it is not locked though you wish it were.
I don't see how this is helping.
Now what do you see?
I see many doors Lord, all shut

Yes my child. You shut the doors on these emotions many years ago. Some are easier to reach, the ones stored in the boxes, but for the rest you feel they will swallow you up and consume you if you were to even stand at the open door.

If you are trying to encourage me it's not working.

I am showing you the truth my dearest child. Only when you face this truth can we begin.

But isn't this what I believe rather than the truth? Wouldn't it be better to show me the real truth?

Yes my child you begin to see. Shall we look again?

Ok.

So He opened the same door again.

Now what do you see?

Another room stacked high with boxes, there are a lot of boxes but the black hole is gone.

There is much for you to face my child but it is not endless and it will not swallow you up. That is the truth. What you saw before is the lie of the enemy which would keep you from even beginning to face these things.

Yes, so is this the room of my emotions, the ones I've not faced.

Yes my child.

It's big and there are lots of doors.

Yes but it is not endless

No. The boxes, are they different memories?

Most of the boxes contain the emotions from specific events my dearest child. Some contain other things.

Another time yes?

Another time my child but come there is a door I wish to open now. Will you allow me to open it?

What is it?

You know.

My feelings about you?

Yes my child. Shall we open it together?

What will happen?

Trust me.

Ok, let's open it.

So we both put our hands on the doorknob and pulled the door open.

Er, did I get that right? This is all a bit weird you know.

Describe it.

Well when we pulled the door open there was a smell, not a nice one and then I kind of saw the room but it seemed to shift and move and there was a wailing sound and the door was sucked shut.

What is in that room wants to remain hidden my child, it wants you to be afraid to approach it, it wants you to disbelieve in its existence. It will resist you entering. There is much in that room that does not want to be disturbed and will try everything to dissuade you from entering.

You make it sound like there are demons in there Lord.

This room is guarded my dearest child. They have not left it untended

That was what I smelt? Demons?

Yes my child. Do you wish to enter?

Lord you know this is kind of stretching me a little in terms of do I actually believe this is happening.

Yes my child I know but I am teaching you of the reality of the spiritual world. I ask only that you trust me and follow.

Ok, Well I will go in because I know I must but you please come with me because you need to get rid of those things. Please.

You wish them to leave?

Yes I do.

If they leave then you will see the truth. Your feelings about me that have been hidden and disguised for so long will be there for you to see.

But I have to see the truth don't I? Yes let's do it.

Hold onto my hand my dearest child and trust me. Do not doubt what you will see but trust me to show you the truth. Are you ready?

Yes.

So we went into this dark room and everything starting flying about and it was like a whirlwind with me and Jesus stood in the middle. I was holding onto Him. Light began to come from Jesus, blinding light and there was a fair bit of wailing and He told them to leave. I felt them leave, and then there was quiet and peace and everything was still and the light was dim but it wasn't dark.

You made that look easy.

I am the Lord.

Yes. You are.

Now tell me what you see.

Well actually its mostly empty, there are a few boxes but not that many.

You see my child the enemy wanted to deceive you into thinking there was so much more here than there actually is.

But you said Lord that there is hate and fear here.

Yes my child so there is but now we can begin to see it for what it is.

We have to unpack the boxes?

One by one my child. Are you willing?

Yes but not now please Lord. I think that's' enough for now.

Yes my child that is enough. We will come again when you are ready.

Ok, it doesn't seem so big and so scary now.

I am in control of all things my dearest child.

That was all very weird but then everything is weird.

To you it seems so.

Yes but help me to accept what you show me and to learn because I want to learn.

Yes my child I will continue to guide and teach you.

As we learned more, he was able to give us more choices and teach us more about the kingdom and what it means to choose healing. We didn't always understand it all of course, I still don't but we were learning and growing, not just healing, with every choice that was made.

Our healing hasn't just been about the trauma of the past but about learning to live in the truth. The truth of who we are and who God is and the truth of the spiritual kingdom that is all around us and within us, to see it as Jesus sees it. So much of our healing has come through our times inside with Jesus or the Holy Spirit or with daddy God. They healed us and taught about the reality of the kingdom at the same time.

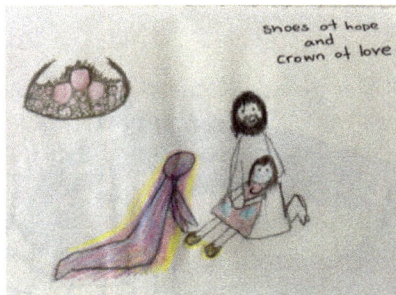

shoes of hope and crown of love

When AJ was learning who she was Jesus and the Holy Spirit gave her a crown of love and shoes of hope. They spoke through those things to tell her who she was and to help her to be that person.

So, I snuggled myself down in Jesus' arms and He held me and kissed my head. I could feel things happening and I cried a bit. I could see the Holy Spirit washing my legs and my feet and I thought this was so strange I might be making it up. But Jesus reassured me and then I looked, and I saw the Holy Spirit putting gold sparkly slippers on my feet and then He put a golden crown on my head. I didn't understand so I asked Jesus and then I saw that they were shoes of hope and the Holy Spirit said that from now on I will walk in hope. And then he said that it was a crown of love and He showed it to me. It is made of gold, but kind of very fine twisted gold made in the shape of leaves maybe I am not sure. It is a like a tiara shape. And I saw that there were tiny pink stones in it, like pink diamonds maybe? And three big ones at the front- one from the father, one from the son and one from the Holy Spirit. It hurt so much that I told Jesus to stop but He held me close and said He would help me bear it. Jesus said that I must always wear my shoes of hope and my crown of love. I cried a very lot.

Jesus showed us the truth of who are to him, as individuals. For Aj it was her crown of love, her shoes of hope and a little later her dress of living daisies. For me it was my crown of suffering.

Well I have my crown Jesus. Is it a crown of suffering?
Yes my little one it is.
What does that mean?
It means my little one that you have suffered greatly but that suffering has not overcome you instead it has become something beautiful and powerful. Something to be worn with joy my little one because of all that I will do through it.
I have a dancing dress Jesus that has pearls on it and little heart shaped rosebuds, that is from Blossum and dolly four and is about your love and about life and becoming and growing. And there are my dancing shoes, not like Blossum's shoes, but they have gold speckles on them. Because I dance with hope I suppose.

Yes my little one and you are dressed in white because I have made you pure and clean and your hair is golden because it reflects my glory.
What does that mean Jesus?
It is like a crown my little one, one which is given to you so that you can show people who I am.
So showing people who you are is a gift Jesus.
Yes my little one it is.
And that is how you see me Jesus.
Yes my little one. You are my Pearl. That is how I see you.

Seeing myself as Jesus sees me is the truth, healing truth, because it sets me free from the lies of the enemy. It sets me free to be who I truly am, which is true healing,

When Jesus was healing and blending the dollies, Aj, Blossum, dolly 4 and dolly 5, he helped us all understand what he was doing. He showed us the golden locket he wears around his neck, so that we are always close to his heart.

In the worship I was in Jesus arms like I often am in the worship time. Sometimes I seem very small and sometimes bigger. I have thought that was strange and it made me think maybe I was just imagining being in Jesus arms but this morning I realized what it is. I am seeing the two parts of me, dolly number two and dolly number three. Dolly number two is older and bigger than dolly number three. I realized that is why sometimes I am big and sometimes I am small in his arms. I saw something else too. I saw the golden locket he wears round his neck which is my heart. I saw the side of it that I never noticed before. It has three layers, a bit like a sandwich. The middle part, like the filling of the sandwich is much thicker than the outside bread parts. I think that this is the three parts of me. Dolly number two, three and four, all together but separate. And dolly number three, that is the child part of me...that is the biggest part. Dolly number two and dolly number four are just little parts of me. Dolly number four is the part that holds the bad memories if you forgot. So I saw that and understood what it means. I want all those parts to be together Mr Mike, but they aren't not yet. I was snuggled in Jesus arms and I felt safe and loved and he kissed the palm of my hand and I cried because I felt so safe and loved. So that was my worship time at church.

As we healed and they blended together he showed us the changes in the locket which helped us all to see and understand what he was doing. It helped us see the progress that was being made too. It gave us hope and helped us to trust in what Jesus was doing to make us whole.

In the worship time I was in Jesus arms and we were dancing. I like that very much Mr Mike. I love to be with him. I saw something I thought was strange. I saw the locket round his neck and the top and middle layer were still merging like I saw last time, that is dolly 2 and dolly 3 (me) but the bottom layer, dolly4, looked more separate than it was before, I could see a gap between that layer and the middle one. I thought that was strange, so I asked Jesus and he told me he was repositioning her? Maybe her I don't know but kind of like he had separated us so he could put her into a better position ready for putting us back together. I still thought that was strange but that's what I thought he said.

Even if we didn't always understand completely what he was showing us it helped us to trust that we were moving forward and that he was in control. It helped us see the reality that was hidden from us, outside life couldn't help us see any of these things most of the time.

When he was blending the alters, he took us inside so that we could see and understand what was happening and so they could choose.

When we got to the meeting place in the evening, we started to feel the Holy Spirit straight away even before it started. When we were worshipping, I was on Jesus knee with dolly 4 and I knew what was going to happen. I cried Mr Mike because it seemed sad to me, but Jesus held me and told it me was a good thing. Me and dolly 4 kind of hugged and it was like she melted into me and then it was just me on Jesus knee. He told me over and over that it was a good thing. I saw my dress Mr Mike and it was like Jesus said. It is daisies and little pink rosebuds and it is very pretty, and I got blonde bits in my hair too.

Jesus and the Holy Spirit have taken us to many different places in the spirit to help us see and understand the healing that was happening so that we could make the choice to let down the walls that we had built up trying to keep safe. So that we could accept the path they had for us. It was always our choice.

My little one my dearest little one the pain is not endless no matter how it seems to you. You are moving forward my little one and though it seems endless to you it is not. Let me take you by the hand my little one and show you something you have not yet seen or understood. Something which will help you take the next step.
Ok.
What do you see my little one?
I see the city. The one you keep showing me.
Yes my little one what else do you see?
It is surrounded by a ring of fire. Big flames.
What do you think that is my little one?
I don't know. It depends where the fire is from. Is it from you or the

enemy?

It is my fire my little one.

Well I suppose I'm thinking of refiners' fire. Maybe something I have to get through to go into the city.

Yes my little one. It is not possible for you to enter the city without going through the fire.

Why?

Because the fire will remove everything that would hinder you there. Everything that would prevent you from reaching out to those in the darkness and leading them to the light.

Haven't I been through enough fire Jesus? I don't want to go. Just leave me...Crying.

No my little one I will not leave you. I did not bring you here to discourage you, but you help you see what I am doing. I am not leading you into the fire my little one you are already in it. But it is not endless my little one.

Tell me you are taking me across the ring and not walking me around it.

We are going across my little one.

It doesn't matter Jesus. I am tired of believing in the city.

Do you think I should keep you in the fire my little one?

I don't know. You put me here.

Why my little one? Why have I led you into the fire?

I know the answer in my heart is you brought me here to punish me.

When I was led into the desert and tempted in every way was that to punish me my little one?

No. It was to make you ready. So you could face what was ahead. So your will would be strong enough and you wouldn't give up or give in.

Yes my little one. Why I have I led you into the fire?

To make me ready. I am tired of believing these things Jesus...

But that does not make them untrue my little one. My little one I have led you into the fire not to punish you but to make you ready. I have brought you here to heal you and make you stronger. To teach you the things you need to learn. To prepare you in all the ways that you need to be prepared so that you can go down into the city and do and be everything you were created for. It is not endless my little one. There is a purpose and a plan and everything I am doing is good.

Ok...Crying.

So my little one even though you are in pain and you do not see or understand what I am doing much of the time will you continue to walk

with me? To have hope for the future I have promised you. To allow me into the places that most need my healing and my love. To trust me and not give up hope. This is just for a little time my dearest one and I am with you in it all.

I don't know if I can...Crying.

You can my little one. I would not ask it of you otherwise.

Often what he was showing us seemed difficult and painful but somehow seeing it gave us the strength to keep moving forward when things got very difficult or painful. One of the most important of those places he has taken me is the garden. The garden which is my heart. I have seen him transform it from something that was cold and dead into a beautiful garden that is full of life.

Hi Holy Spirit.

Hello my little one. Will you come into the garden with me?

Yes. Are you going to show me something?

Yes my little one I am.

Oh it is very bright and warm here now.

Yes my little one for we are thawing out the ground which has been frozen and barren for so very long. As the angels dig, they are uncovering what lies beneath my little one.

Is that what you want me to see?

Yes my little one it is.

It is just a big black hole covered by black frozen soil.

Yes my little one it is but the hole is not empty.

Oh dear. That sounds bad.

But we are able my little one to bring healing to every part of you. Do not be afraid. Are you willing to see what is there my little one?

If it will help me.

Yes my little one it will. Come then.

We climbed down a silver rope ladder into a deep dark cave. It seems pretty empty to me.

But it is not my little one. Look at your feet.

They are sinking. It is like black ooze. It is smelly.

Yes my little one it is.

Sorry. I am just wanting to run away.

But we are here with you my little one.

I know. So, I am thinking this is like an infection and this is like disgusting pus, but I don't know what it is except it is a bad thing to have in my heart.

Yes my little one but now this place has been uncovered we can begin to heal it.

68

I suppose this black stuff is the anger I am feeling, and it comes from an infected wound which you want to heal.

Yes my little one it does.

And daddy wants to fill this place with his love when it is healed and cleaned.

Yes my little one this part of the garden will be made new.

That's all good but you need to get rid of this goo and get to the hurt it is covering.

Yes my little one that is what we are going to do. My little one the anger that you are feeling covers a deep wound. It is a wound that only the love of the father can heal. He is wanting to fill you with his love my dearest one so that your heart is made whole and well again.

So why are you showing me this?

So that you can understand and not be afraid my little one. So that we can heal you and set you free from the pain and the loneliness that is in your heart. So that we can fill you with the love that you so desperately need.

Well yes but I don't know what to do.

You do not need to do anything my little one except trust us. I know my dearest one that to be angry is frightening to you, but we will hold you and enable you and when the anger has been released you will be able to see the wound that lies beneath it. Then we can begin to heal that wound my little one. It will take a little time but not too long my little one.

It took months and much healing but when he took me back the garden was being transformed, just like he said it would be.

We are changing you from the inside out. As the water from the fountain reaches into the garden you will see the changes my little one. Come. Let me show you what we have done.

Ok.....It is very beautiful Jesus. It looks like the waterfall water except it is going up and not down.

It is welling up inside of you my little one and it will not ever stop. It is here to bring you life and through you to others.

You said I would know better who I am and be more secure in that.

Yes my little one I did. Look at the garden my little one. Look what is happening.

Little blue flowers everywhere covering where the ground was bare.

Yes my little one what do you think they are?

Truth maybe.

Yes my little one the truth is reaching into every part of your garden.

No part will be left untouched. **My dearest little one you have been filled with who we are. Our father's love poured out my little one not in a way you have known before but deeper far, far deeper, reaching into places where you cannot see my little one but where it will change you.** You did say it would be different.
Yes my little one I did.

It has helped me understand, it has helped me follow, it has given me the hope and strength that I needed when the healing was really hard and seemed endless. It has helped me understand the things of the spirit and how the things on the outside are connected to what is happening on the inside. It has helped me understand that healing is far more than it appears to be. It has helped me see the truth that is written all through the bible but is often hidden from us because often we don't understand the things of the spirit. It has not only been healing from the past but has drawn me further into the truth, which is just another kind of healing.

Hi Holy Spirit
Hello my dearest little one.
I am thinking about baptism and blending. It is a different way to see it, but it makes sense to me.
Yes my little one as your spirit and ours become more deeply entwined, more deeply connected, we become more as one my little one. There is less separation between us.
So like having the mind of Christ and being led by the spirit and being rooted and established in love and all of those things, going deeper into your heart. That is all blending with you.
Yes my little one it is and just as in the blending with alters the distinction between us grows less, you become more and more like Jesus, though you remain who you are my little one.
Just like the alters are still who they are but people see me mostly.
Yes my little one and the more the blending progresses the more people will see Jesus and the less they will see you.
And that is already started. It starts when I got saved and accepted Jesus into my heart.
Yes my little one and the more you open up your heart to us the more the blending progresses.
I was thinking how when Jesus was baptized all his doors were open, and you could just go in completely and fill him up to overflowing.
Yes my little one there were no closed doors in his heart. I could fill every part of him my little one just as I long to do with you.

70

I am thinking that maybe for a lot of people they have a lot of closed doors and maybe you can't get very far in at all and that is why there doesn't seem too much difference and they aren't changed, obviously anyway.

Yes my little one that is so but we are always working to help them open up their hearts to us, just as we are with you.

And my heart Holy Spirit, I don't suppose I will have all my doors open to you because I think there will be more you need to do maybe but this time is for me to allow you to open up as much as I can so that when it is time then you can go deep and the blending [with Jesus] can be more.

Yes my little one that is so.

I want that Holy Spirit.

Yes my little one I know you do.

Well I don't know how but you do.

Spend time with us my little one, allow us access, keep choosing us in everything. In that way we will have access to those areas of your heart that are most needed. My little one you are right in thinking that there will be more. There will be many more times of blending and filling for you, but this time is special my little one. It is worth preparing for. It will make many things possible for you that are not possible now.

Yes. I see that.

Sometimes he has healed me by showing me things that weren't painful at all and by spending time with me having fun or just showing me things that encouraged me.

This afternoon I decided I just needed to spend some time with the Holy Spirit, not to hear anything or do anything just to be with him. So, I put on some worship music. I had a lovely time. I did some dancing with Jesus. Heaven seemed to turn into a disco with rainbow lights. It made me laugh and cry and the same time. And I spent time with daddy in the soft pillows and I was kind of surrounded by space and shooting stars and the Holy Spirit was swirling round us like a gold sparkly comet. It reminded me that they aren't stressed or sad. That it's all under control and that I'm so loved. I cried a lot, but it was good, and I felt better.

Jesus has taken me on a journey inside and shown me many things to bring me healing and hope and to teach me about the spirit. They have taught me who I am and who they are, Father, Son and Holy Spirit. Spending time inside with each of them has helped me understand that I am safe and loved at all times. They have

71

helped me see the healing that is happening in my heart and to keep walking forward no matter how painful. Seeing and understanding the things of the kingdom has given me hope when there was nothing to see on the outside, the hope that I needed to keep on walking. The things I have learned aren't just for me but because of what he wants to do through me. To help his children discover who he is and who they are and how to live in the true reality of the kingdom.

My little one when I made you I made you with a purpose. You were sent into this world to show the lost and the broken who I am. That much has not been hidden my little one. It has been visible from the beginning and the enemy has worked hard to destroy both you and your purpose in this world. But there is more my little one for you are not only sent to reveal who I am to this world but to bring my presence and my power, to bring my love and hope in a new way. To bring understanding the things of the spirit, to teach my people many mysteries. To open the eyes of the spiritually blind and open the ears of the spiritually deaf my little one. I am sending you into my church to bring change and reformation. That is who you are my little one. You are my Pearl born out of suffering, redeemed at great price and sent out to bring hope and healing and life my little one.

Chapter 8

A Whole New World

When we first learned about the inside world that the alters lived in we weren't sure that we believed it but over time we came to accept it as real and true, a place that Jesus created for the alters to live in when they weren't at the surface. It wasn't just that though. There were places inside that were ruled over by the enemy, places where alters were hidden or imprisoned, places of fear and of darkness and pain. Jesus took me to the inside world a lot of times. First of all, I went with Blossum, before I knew I existed, but eventually I went as me. That was the place where I first gave myself to Jesus, in the stream where he took me many times.

I sat down with my feet in the water and Jesus stood in the stream and gently took hold of my feet and started to wash them clean.

My little one all the cares of this world are not meant to be carried by you. I am the only one you need. I will care for you and love you and keep you safe. I will love you and carry you through the darkness. These are my promises to you and I will keep them. Will you accept them my little one. Will you accept me?

I jumped into his arms and cried and cried and he held me. And all the children gathered around us and started to pray for me and I cried so much I thought I wouldn't ever stop.

Jesus I'm so sorry.

I know my little one I know that you are. Keep your eyes fixed on me my little one and do not listen to lies. They have no place in your heart for your heart belongs to me. Rest now and do not be afraid my little one. You are safe and you are loved and will always be so.

The inside realty that seemed so strange at first became as real to me as the outside. Even though I didn't see it as clearly as I wanted to somehow, I always knew what I was seeing or hearing or touching, just like with my physical senses. Jesus was teaching me, or the Holy Spirit was, how to use my spiritual senses.

Reality is not defined by your ability to discern it my little one. Reality is what I say it is. It is, regardless of your ability to see hear feel or sense it. Reality does not change according to your perception of it my little one but I am helping you to see and perceive true reality not according to your natural senses my little one but according to the spirit which is given to you in full measure. Learning to see and hear

and sense the things of the spirit takes time my little one and it also takes faith. You will be fully equipped for the life that you will lead. A life of love and hope and joy and service to me my little one and that is what matters most of all.

It is Jesus?

My little one you are my delight. I will not ever let you go. All the things that are ahead for you are in my hands. I am making you able to live the life I have for you my little one in many ways that you have not seen or understood. Keep following and do not doubt my love for you. You are my Pearl, precious and beloved in every way and no matter how difficult the path I lead you on that remains my little one. It does not change. If the path is difficult it is only because you are willing my little one and your willingness allows me to do so much more through your life. Be content to follow then my little one trusting in who I am and not in your own understanding. I am able to do all things my little one even the things I have promised you.

Through my visits to the inside world Jesus wanted me to learn and to understand about the reality of the spiritual and how people don't need bodies to be real. The alters inside were every bit as real as people outside. They had bodies that could be hurt even though they weren't physical bodies but spiritual ones. I still have a lot more to learn about this. Jesus took me inside for many reasons. He took me inside to teach me about the spiritual things, about their reality and to help me learn how to see and hear and feel in the spirit. He took me inside to meet with other alters and to hear their stories, which was also my story. He took me inside to make friends and to witness his provision and healing for the alters who lived there. He took me inside so that I could help him to rescue alters who were lost or held captive by the enemy. He took me inside to learn about his authority over the enemy, how to follow his instructions and to witness spiritual battles firsthand.

What are you doing little girl? Do you think you can take them from here? They belong to me.

No. No they don't. And I will take them from here. They belong to Jesus not to you. He has come to save them.

Has he how nice. But all I see is you little girl. You can't save them. No one can.

The Lord Jesus can and he has come. I am not alone. The four Angels appeared next to me with their swords.

Neither am I.

74

Then others came out of hiding it seemed like lots of them. They were like a dark cloud surrounding me and the Angels. We were a bit outnumbered but then Jesus was there.

Enough be gone dark ones. These are my children and you shall not keep them any longer.

They screamed and kind of melted through the walls and they were gone. Then Jesus spoke to the alters who were still on the ground looking scared…

All of it was to help me grow and learn, to understand his path of healing, to discover the truth of my story and to heal from the things that were done to us. He wanted me to understand the system of alters I was a part of and where I fitted. He wanted to help us learn to work together and learn together and heal together.

He also taught me a lot about my own spiritual land, that each of us has our own spiritual land the reflects our heart or soul. He had taken me to see part my own land, what I knew as level five, parts that were a desert or a wasteland, but which were now coming back to life. Like it says:

Forget the former things;
do not dwell on the past.
See, I am doing a new thing!
Now it springs up;
do you not perceive it?
I am making a way in the wilderness
and streams in the wasteland.
The wild animals honor me,
the jackals and the owls,
because I provide water in the wilderness
and streams in the wasteland,
to give drink to my people, my chosen...

Isaiah 43:18-20

He showed me how he was transforming my land as I healed and also how as the alters blended with me that my land and theirs were joined. I am sure I have a lot more to learn about these things, about the mysteries that are hidden in these truths and how we as his children are so much more than we understand ourselves to be.

Hello Jesus.
Hello my little one.

Yesterday was interesting Jesus but I would like to understand more.

Yes my little one I know that you would. Ask me your questions my little one.

Mostly I am wondering about level five if that's what it is. Is it a level...it seems different somehow.

Level five is different my little one because it is your land. It is the description of your life and all that is contained within it.

I know that lots of things on the inside are like metaphors Jesus. Is it like that, like the desert and the wilderness?

Yes my little one it is like that but the land is real, nevertheless. My little one it is true that all of the land belongs to you for it was taken from you and will be given back to you but the levels that are currently occupied by the alters are given to them my little one for their survival and protection and now for their healing.

But they and the land came from me.

Yes my little one they did and they will be given back to you in time.

So all of the inside world will go?

In time my little one yes for it will not be needed anymore.

But is level five different Jesus?

Yes my little one for that is your land. Everyone has their own spiritual landscape my little one even those who do not have a spiritual world as such.

So the spiritual world is like the inside I mean, is an extension of my spiritual landscape.

Yes my little one that is so. All of it has come from you my little one from what was given to you in the beginning.

So will the other levels kind of blend with level five, like when alters blend.

Yes my little one the land will be given back to you just as the alters will be given back to you in time.

So none of the other alters can go into my land?

No my little one they can't.

So do, does every alter have their own spiritual landscape like I do?

Yes my little one they do. The difference is that yours is connected to and holds together all the other levels. That is not so for the others my little one. They may have some connections to other levels and places but not in quite the same way.

So when I blended with like Jennifer did I get her spiritual landscape?

Yes my little one it was returned to you just as she was returned to

you.
And that is part of making me stronger.
Yes my little one it is for as your own spiritual land grows stronger and begins to flourish so do you.
Because we are connected.
Yes my little one you are part of the land and the land is part of you.
I am thinking about the physical world and body Jesus. Is it the same there?
Yes my little one you are connected spiritually and physically to the land. What is true on the inside is also true on the outside. Little one you are healing and growing in many ways. The ground which belongs to you is also beginning to flourish my little one for as the water flows out into the land everything comes to life.
And it is all a picture of something else but more than that.
Yes my little one the desert of waste is a picture of the years that have been lost to you but it is also a real and tangible place which affects your life and the life of those inside. My little one the spiritual places which belong to you, that land which is yours is being reclaimed. For a long time it was occupied by the enemy my little one but that is no longer true. The enemy is gone my little one and now my spirit can begin to fill the land bringing life and hope and joy. What is true on the inside is also true on the outside my little one for as his life fills you on the inside it will overflow to the outside. Your life will change my little one and begin to blossom and flourish in the same way as the inside.
So are you saying the desert was once occupied by the enemy?
Yes my little one he had many encampments in the land that belongs to you but no longer my little one. He is gone.
So...but he is still in some places like level four?
Yes my little one the inside world is not yet fully cleansed. There is still much healing to do.
Ok. So now my land is cleansed and water can flow into the rest that helps, it puts you there, your life I suppose.
Yes my little one it does and the process of healing is accelerated in those places.
Ok. So you said what happens in the inside land affects my land.
Yes my little one it does but not to the same degree. Those places which still belong to the enemy or are under his influence can make the healing process in your own land more difficult but they cannot prevent it. The things that he pours out cannot enter your land my little one for it is protected and kept clean by my spirit who is present at all times.

So how is it made more difficult?

Because of the connections that exist my little one. It is like shock waves or vibrations which pass from one place to another. Each place is affected to a greater or lesser degree my little one. Sometimes the effect will be small and at other times greater but it can still be felt.

So when level four is sorted out everything will be better.

Yes my little one it will.

Ok. I think I am kind of understanding Jesus. It is a bit hard to get hold of but I kind of get it.

My little one the inside world is beginning to heal just as the alters that live there are beginning to heal. They are connected my little one and not separate. Your own land is also healing as you do. Each affects the other my little one and your land affects the inside lands bringing healing and restoration there also.

That's good then Jesus.

Yes my little one it is very good.

As I healed and blended with the alters inside their land began to change and it grew smaller. This was because the land was being given back to me just as Jesus said. With the last blending done it was time for the inside world to be given back to me, to be my land once again. It was an ending but a beginning also.

He took me up the mountain so I could see out over the land.

Tell me what you see my little one.

The mountain is so beautiful. It is covered in flowers. There is just the dell and the little stream left Jesus. And empty huts. There is no one there.

No my little one none now remain for they are all given back to you. My little one as the land is given back to you the healing that we have been doing for so very long will be completed. There is more my little one but this part is ended.

As I watched it was kind of like water came up through the ground and it all disappeared into a beautiful golden mist that was filled with rainbows, and the mist got higher and higher until it reached us at the top of the mountain and then I was back outside.

Chapter 9

The Path of Truth.

Before Jesus could even begin to heal the past, we had to accept that it was true, to see it for what it was. Accepting the truth of the past was so painful and frightening that we didn't want to do it, not any of us. It was easier to keep hiding in the darkness than to face the truth of what had happened to us. There was so much grief and loss to be faced that it was overwhelming, we could only do it with Jesus because we didn't have the strength.

My little one I am here. Do not be anxious but trust what I am showing you.
Well I saw the park. I was there with mum. We went for a lolly and sat in the café bit which was cool. Did I see that right?
Yes my little one that is what I showed you but there is more. Are you willing to see?
Help me to be willing. I don't feel willing.
My little one you know who I am.
Yes. I know you love me and want to heal me. I'm sorry. Have your way Jesus.
Come then my little one and allow me to show you the truth.
I'm afraid.
Yes my little one I know you are but I am here. I will not leave you.
Ok then. Show me.

It was such a struggle for me to allow myself to see but it was just the same. She handed me over to a man who led me away into the woods. I didn't see anymore. I was overwhelmed by grief.
My little one I understand your grief. I am here with you.
I don't want to see any more of this stuff why must I see?
I want you to know the truth my little one. Do not fear it for it leads to healing and freedom.
Jesus I don't understand. I know you keep saying I will eventually but how do I understand that. How?
My little one your mum was caught in a trap she did not know how to escape. Like you she had many ways of protecting herself from the truth. This enabled her to do and to be many things that are difficult for you to understand. This did not mean that she didn't love you in her own way for she did but there were so many conflicts for her and so much fear my little one that she failed you and betrayed you as should not have been done.

I don't want to accept any of this.
I know my little one, but this is the truth.
I just want to hide I don't want any of this to be true. Please...
My little one I know you are in great pain. Let me come and comfort you my little one. Rest in my arms a while. I will enable you to continue, to take the next step my dearest one. That is all you must do.

It wasn't just a battle with our own hearts, trying to avoid facing the pain but it was a battle with the enemy too. They didn't want the truth to be known because they understood that it opened the door to healing and freedom to us. They challenged the truth at every point. They tried desperately hard for years to convince us that the bad things never happened, that they couldn't have happened. We fought this same battle over and over for a very long time. They wanted the truth to stay hidden, for us to live in denial of what had happened because then Jesus couldn't heal the bad things, he couldn't set us free and we couldn't fulfil his plans and purposes for us. The battle was fierce and was fought over and over again.

Hello Mike
I think it started last night, it's difficult to be sure because this stuff goes on in my head all the time but it seems so intense at the moment its making me cry... it's like all the stuff that ever causes me to stumble but all at once. So there's.. none of this is real, you are just making it up, there was no abuse you are just sick, there are no alters you are just mad... and you can't trust any of the things you've heard, how do you know any of it was Jesus, you just made it up, none of it is true... and you are all alone, no-one will help you, nobody really cares, mike won't ever help you, you are on your own... and there is no hope, you'd be better off dead, this can't ever be made right, you are too damaged and nobody would care, nobody would miss you, you could end it right now and it would all be over... and look at you, you are a waste of space, you are nothing, you are selfish, unkind..etc etc... all with a smattering of 'is God real anyway?', your life is nothing, it will never amount to anything, it will be this way forever.... you get the idea. I am so tired.. I spent some time praying this afternoon.. I use the term loosely....it was me crying, trying to speak out truth, telling Jesus that I love Him and that even if it kills me I will trust Him.. all mixed in with a lot of help mes ... and I got an image or a picture in my mind. I was walking along a very narrow path, so narrow there was really only room for me to walk on it. Along the edges of the

path on both sides, so well within touching distance of me, were what seemed like scores of demons all leering and shouting and clawing at me.. and in front me, just out of reach was Jesus beckoning me on, drawing me on, encouraging me to walk forward but always staying just out of reach so I had to keep walking if I wanted to reach Him. I don't know how accurate that is, whether it was just my imagination but it reminds me that I all I have to do it keep my focus on Him and keep walking as He leads, because the enemy can't stop me, he can only try to make me give up walking.

Jesus spoke to us in ways that we could understand. He gave us pictures and visions to help us see when words alone wouldn't have been enough or maybe would have got lost in all the 'noise'. They became part of 'normal' life for us. They helped us survive.

When we finally accepted that the bad things were true, that they had happened, the battle grew fiercer elsewhere. We were trusting and depending on Jesus for everything, we needed to hear his voice. We spent hours with him every day while he healed and comforted us and taught us about the spiritual world. The enemy wanted to cause doubt and confusion so that we wouldn't trust what we heard, or the things that we saw. So, we wouldn't continue to follow and to learn, to become all that Jesus had for us to be. They began to trick us, more and more, pretending to be Jesus, so that we heard their voice and not his. So, we saw what they wanted us to see. So that we would be confused and unsure and ultimately lose hope and be destroyed.

Their biggest target was his promises, most of all his promise to take us to America, to have a new life and to fulfil all that he had for us. They tricked us over and over convincing us it was almost time to leave, telling us of all the plans and the wonderful things that were ahead. Causing us to stall in our healing, lose focus on Jesus and ultimately to stop trusting what we heard. That was devastating to us. We couldn't understand why Jesus had allowed it. Why had he let them trick us? Why hadn't he told us? Of course, he had, over and over but we wanted to hear what we were being told more than we wanted the truth. It was a hard lesson to learn but we did learn it.

Confusion

My little one the lie that you believed brought you much pain for that is what lies do. My dearest one living in the truth is the only way for you to truly live. I know my little one that you do not understand why I allowed this to happen, why I allowed the enemy to hurt you so but my dearest one I was with you. My truth was always with you if you had but chosen to see it. My little one the enemy knows your weaknesses for he created them. He wants to destroy you my little one and he will use his lies to do this if he can. But I am greater my little one. The truth of who I am will sustain you through any lie and any deceit. My love will overcome everything that he has done my little one. I did not allow this because I do not care my little one I allowed it because I knew that I could work through it to accomplish many things my little one. I allowed it because I knew that I could use it to help set you free from the very thing that he was trying to destroy you with. My dearest one this is not yet easy for you to see and for you it is still painful and confusing but I see my little one. I see so many things. This time will pass but the memory of this time will remain with you always. The things that you have learned and will learn through this will remain with you my little one and they will protect you in the future when the enemy is trying to deceive you and lead you away from the path that I have for you. My little one my love for you has not and will not ever fail. Though the enemy will hurt you many times I am always with you my little one and I will always redeem everything that he does. He cannot win my little one, not if you keep your trust and your hope in me and in who I am.

Jesus used everything the enemy did to draw us closer to him, to show us the true destructive nature of lies and the freedom that comes with the truth, even if it's not what we want to hear. He showed us the cunning and the cruelty of the enemy. He showed us how important it is to be wise and to be wary. We still made many mistakes. I still make mistakes, but they aren't so devastating to me because I know that's what they are. They don't change who Jesus is. They don't change his love for me or his plans. He is always able to work all things for my good no matter how many times I mess up.

Jesus healed the pain and the trauma of the past, taking us back into the memories of the bad things, holding us and comforting us, showing us the truth of the life, we had lived collectively, but we have needed more than this. Along with the pain and the trauma, the past held us bound in the lies of the enemy so that we couldn't see or accept the truth about ourselves or about Jesus. Breaking those bonds and setting us free has been a battle. A battle against all the lies and the deceptions of the enemy and all the things that held us bound which we couldn't even see. The path that leads to the truth is a path that has to be walked with Jesus because he is the one who fights out battles for us. He gives us the strength and the ability to stand and to make the choices that need to be made. He is the truth. Not only that but he gives us the protection we need, angels who fight on our behalf when we are surrounded by the enemy. He has led us forward on our path of truth, the path to freedom even though it has often felt like each step taken was an unwinnable battle.

The presence of the Lord is with you. Do not fear. You are in the midst of a mighty battle but the Lord is fighting for you. Stay strong in him. Trust him and you will see a new day. It will be a day of victory for the Lord is doing a mighty thing. Stand strong then and wait on the Lord who is your defender. He will not leave you abandoned but will rescue you with his mighty arm of victory. Do not be afraid.
I didn't see him but I think it was an angel.

Jesus began by showing us the lies that were holding us. We didn't see them, we didn't know they were even there. They didn't seem like lies to us. We thought they were the truth.

Tell me what you believe about yourself.
Lord....crying
I will enable you, are you willing?
I want to be willing.
That is enough.
I don't know if I can do it Lord. Everything gets stuck you know and I definitely don't want to know.
You wish to keep running from the truth.

Yes.

I am truth, if you run from the truth you run from me.

Oh dear. You will have to help me Jesus. There's nothing there right now. I mean nothing.

I know what is there. Do not worry I can do all things, can I not?

Yes.

Then begin.

Well you said yesterday that I believe I am nothing and I can see that's true, that I don't matter, that the fact of my existence makes no difference to anyone.

You think they don't care whether you live or die?

Yes… and no. In my head I see that isn't true because obviously my children love me and need me and my friends, well I suppose they would miss me but..

Go on.

If I had died before, you know, if you had let me die rather than helping me to survive…

Would that make any difference?

Yes, I suppose.

That is because you do not understand anything of the impact you have had or the impact you will have, that will make a difference for all eternity.

Lord I can't believe anything that I do is that significant.

I told you, you don't understand, continue.

Then help me Lord because there's nothing there, except fear.

My child the doors are unlocked and open already you have only to go in.

Show me how.

Take my hand.

I saw myself taking his hand and he led me through a door into a dark room. The only thing I could see clearly was a baby, naked and lying on the floor, crying. There were lots of other things in the room which I couldn't see with my eyes but…I am unloved and unlovable I am alone, no-one cares for me, I am vulnerable and unprotected. I am not worth protecting, crying. I have no rights, no worth. I exist for the pleasure and gratification of others. I belong to no one and no one wants me, except Satan who wants to use me and cause me pain and I must allow him to do that because that is my purpose, to serve Satan by allowing him to do whatever he wants. That is my worth and my purpose. Lord that can't be right surely? I mean how can I live for you with a purpose like that?

Keep looking.

I am an object, not a person, my feelings and opinions do not matter, they do not even exist. I am dirty, shameful, bad, completely corrupt with nothing good in me. Utterly worthless. My life has no good purpose and I can achieve nothing of value, I am waiting to die, that is what I deserve. I am nothing but a pile of shit.

You see my child what you have hidden away, closed the door on and yet what you believe about yourself affects everything.

Can we come out now Lord and shut the door?

We can come out but the door must remain open, these lies will be removed one by one. Only then will the door be shut and sealed so that nothing can ever be put in there again. Remember what I told you. What is in that room is not you, only the lies that you have believed about yourself. That is not who you are.

Then why is it so painful?

Because you still believe it.

How do I manage to even keep living believing all that?

By shutting it away my child and not allowing yourself to acknowledge it. Which is where we began.

Yes. Ok.

Now you have faced this fear and you have seen the lies we can begin to remove them. Are you willing my child?

Yes. What will that mean?

It will mean dealing with the source of those lies, with the memories and experiences that you have buried and shut away. There are many rooms my dearest child that we must enter together.

I will do it Lord, with you, please, I need your help. How can I even bear to look?

I will give you the strength and the courage. Do not be afraid.

Jesus began the long and painful process of replacing the lies that the enemy planted with his truth. It has taken a lot of time because those lies went to the very core of us, of who we believed we were. He had to show us the truth a little at a time and help us to accept it. It was something he had to repeat over and over and over because the lies went so deep and had such a strong hold on us.

Lies that told us we were bad, worthless and didn't deserve to live. Lies that told us we belonged to Satan and that God hated us. Lies that told us we could never be loved or have any of the things we wanted because we are bad. Lies that told us there is no hope for anything better. So many of them, all of them holding us, keeping us from the truth of who we are and who Jesus is.

Ok well right from the beginning I was always told that God hated me because I belonged to Satan and that Satan and his followers were the only ones who could protect me from the wrath of God. I was told that there was no way I could ever escape from that because of what I'd done and because I belonged to Satan. Erm… so Jesus.. who I was told was the one who would come looking for me.. He was the one to be really afraid of because if he found me then he would not only kill me but he would torture me forever because I am evil and so… and they said that because I gave my soul to the devil that Jesus wanted to punish me and that he had ways of doing that.. I have always been afraid of Jesus and always believed that Satan was my only hope, we were told we could avoid being found and tortured by Jesus if we remained faithful and under Satan's protection. That he could keep us alive even after we die and we could go to another place then where Jesus can't get us and we can do whatever we want forever. There was a lot of other stuff too about how in this place we would be the torturers but I don't really want to talk about that.. I suppose now that I've met Jesus and I don't think, I mean he says he loves me and he hasn't hurt me and… but I suppose I'm still afraid of him because I think, well I don't know because of who I am… maybe .. I suppose I think he might change his mind and then there's Satan because I've betrayed him he will get me and then I will die and I don't know what will happen. I'm confused and I'm afraid. Can you help me because I'm not sure anymore. I can't talk about this anymore. Thanks.

Jesus had to break the lies one by one whilst replacing them with the truth of who we are and of who he is. With each new freedom we were able to walk further on the path until we were held once again by a lie that was deep in our heart. A lie that was keeping us from the next step he had for us.

I feel lost and afraid and alone…Crying.

I know you do my little one but those feelings come from deep within from the past my little one. You are not alone my little one. You are never alone.

I am shut in a dark place all alone.

No my little one I am with you and I have come to set you free.

I don't know where I am.

My little one the pain of the past is like a prison that holds you captive. It keeps you from being free to enjoy all the love and friendship that I

am longing to give to you.

But...you have set me free so many times. Why am I still locked in a dark hole.

Because this is a deeper place my little one, one which only the fathers love can set you free from. My little one do not be afraid. He will not ever hurt you.

I feel like I won't ever get out of here.

But that is not so my little one. Will you trust me and follow where I lead?

Crying a lot... Yes. But I can't go anywhere. I am stuck here forever.

No my little one you are not. I am able to lead you into freedom.

How many prisons can I be in Jesus?

My little one the enemy constructed many prisons for you but they are not endless my little one. I will lead you out of all of them.

Learning the truth of who we are has been such an important part of the path Jesus had for us. We had to learn from scratch who we were. When we first remembered the bad things, it rewrote our history. It changed how we saw ourselves, who we believed we were. Nothing was what we thought. Who was this person that all these bad things had happened to, worse who was this person who had done such terrible things, had even given birth to babies we never knew existed? We didn't know who that was. How could that be me? Having alters made it even more confusing. How much of what I remembered was actually me, my memory. Did I do that? Did I choose that? Who am I was our constant thought? It was terrifying. For Aj and Blossum and me we each went through finding out we weren't the person we thought. We all thought we were Jennifer and when finally, I discovered I was me, Pearl, I was afraid for a long time that I would turn out to be someone else. Through all of this, through all of the changes and relearning who I was, Jesus was the one constant. No matter what name I had, no matter what my story was, what had been done to me, what I had done, he told me you are who I say that you are. You are my beloved child. You are safe and you are loved, and nothing can ever change that. Those are the truths that I hold on to, no matter what else changes I now know that to be true.

Jesus became my security and my identity is found in who he says I am. I have had to learn from him who I am because I didn't know. How could I know in all of that confusion and mix of different voices and stories, experiences and memories? The only person who knows who I am is Jesus because he is the one who made me.

My life doesn't tell me who I am. The way people treat me or what they think or say about me doesn't tell me who I am. I have learned to trust who Jesus says I am. He is still showing me who that is. It means my own ideas of who I am don't limit what I think I can do or be. I listen to what Jesus says about that because he knows, I don't. It means he can lead me further down the path he has for me because I'm not hindered by my own ideas of who I am or what I can do. I am who Jesus says I am. I belong to him.

I am who you want me to be here in this life, you made me with a purpose and maybe that's why I am so many in one. I don't know I suppose so. But I am still not sure what it means to be Pearl in his world and I am not even sure what I mean by that really. Maybe I am trying to feel safe in who I am and put limits on who I can be and I don't think you want me to do that. You want me to, I don't know, live without limits because I am in you and you are in me and you don't have limits.

Yes my little one that is so. In trying to define yourself and saying I am this and I am not that you are giving yourself limits and boundaries that I have not given you my little one. You can be whoever you are called to be. You are who I say that you are my little one in any given situation. It does not matter if you think you can't or you're not, in me you can be anyone my little one as I enable you.

But even so, I am me?

Yes my little one you are and even though you can be anyone I call you to be, the person that I will call you to be is you my little one but not your idea of who you are but mine.

Which is a lot bigger.

Yes my little one it is.

I think it would be hard to feel safe in that if I didn't trust you Jesus.

Yes my little one it would but I am helping you to trust me my little one so that you can be all things, just as I enable you to be.

Maybe that is why you keep on changing who I am, or who I think I am, so I don't get stuck in thinking this is what I am and what I can do. I have to say I don't know and maybe I can be that and maybe I can do that because how can I know. I have to trust what you know about me not what I know about me.

Yes my little one you do and what I know about you will always exceed what you know about yourself.

That is true Jesus. So when you say to me that you want me to do something and I think I can't, well I am wrong because you know and I don't.

Yes my little one exactly so and I will often ask you to do things you are not aware that you can do or be but I know my little one. I know everything you are capable of, not in your own strength my little one, but mine.

So I don't need to be anxious about anything you ask me to do because you know I can do it and you aren't ever wrong.

Yes my little one.

I suppose I still might not want to though Jesus but mostly what gets in the way is fear but I don't need to be afraid.

No my little one you don't. Not ever.

Because you know who I am and I don't.

Yes my little one.

So I am Pearl but only you know what that means.

Yes my little one I do but you will also learn what it means my little one just not in the way that you have been thinking.

A different way to see myself.

Yes my little one, not defined as the world defines you but as I define you.

Which is very different.

Yes my little one very different.

And I suppose even though I am not living as Pearl age 9 with my story, somehow I am more than that. I mean that doesn't really say who I am does it. Maybe I have been thinking it does, but it doesn't. Maybe it says something about me I don't know but it doesn't say who I am, and if I think living as that Pearl is living as me, then I am wrong.

Jesus always told me that the purpose of the path was so that I could be the person he made me to be, Pearl Sunshine. It has been so confusing not just to me, but to Aj and Blossom too that we each of us had to keep on living life as Jennifer, to be a grownup woman with two children looking after a house, and for me having a job too. I have thought very often that the path I am on is the exact opposite of what he promised, that it keeps me from being who I am. It has caused me a lot of pain and distress. It has made me feel like I'm irrelevant and might as well not exist. It is lonely and stressful. But I know now that Jesus has been working through it to make me stronger in who he says I am, who I truly am and not who I'm seen as. He has been working through the loneliness, through my all my unmet needs, to give me something more, a relationship with him that is rooted in the truth.

You are still learning to see yourself as I do my little one. You are not

the person you see. I do not see you as you do my little one, I see so much more.

Crying…I don't want to be this person.

My little one do you think that who a person is, is defined by the circumstances they are in?

I think circumstances can limit who they can be and the things they can do.

Circumstances can change the way you see yourself my little one but they cannot change who you are.

I know you see it all different. I don't want my story to have a sad ending. I don't want to give up. But I think that you are making it too hard and I don't understand why I have to be so alone.

So that you can learn who I am my little one through my eyes and not anyone else's. My little one you are my child and my servant and I am preparing you for a life that is so special and so extraordinary that you cannot see or understand it right now. But my little one if I were to give you all the things that you want, the fun and the laughter and the friendships, all good things my little one and not bad, if I gave you those things now then something else would be lost. Something far more precious even than those things my little one.

There is so many things I want to say about that but what would be lost Jesus?

My little one the bond that we have is a special one and not like the one that most people have.

Is it? I don't know.

My little one when you want to ask something who do you come to?

Well when I am doing better I come to you Jesus cos you know all the answers.

Yes my little one I do and when you want to understand something who do you come to?

You.

And when you need guidance or help or love or comfort or healing or hope?

You Jesus because I don't have anyone else.

No my little one you don't and though this causes you pain and distress because you feel lonely and like you are missing out on all the good things life has to offer really I am giving you something far more precious my little one. I am giving you myself.

Can't I have both?

Yes my little one in time you will be able to have both but for now my little one I want your focus to be on me. My little one I can meet all of

90

your needs if you come to me and spend time with me. That is not because I do not want you to have fun and friendships with others my little one only that I need to be first.

But that is the same for everyone Jesus not just for me.

Yes my little one it is my desire for all of my children but not many are willing to pay the price my little one.

I am not willing. It is too hard.

No my little one it is not. My dearest one you have chosen to follow me no matter where I will lead you and to pay the price for that because you know in your heart that there is no other way for you. Nothing else will satisfy you my little one. Nothing else will make the journey worthwhile for you.

If I have really done that why am I crying all the time and wanting to give up.

Because there are many things in this world which will oppose that choice my little one and make it difficult for you but you have made the choice nevertheless and it is only because of that, that I can lead you as I am. It is a difficult path my little one and requires more of you than you know how to give but you do not walk alone my little one. I am with you. I am always with you giving you everything that you need.

I still don't understand.

Only because you do not see as I do my little one. Hold on to me and trust me. Walk through each day with me because that is the best thing you can do. Surrender everything to me my little one and do not be afraid. I am for you my little one in everything no matter how it seems to you, no matter how hard it gets and no matter how far away the promise seems to you.

I don't think I can do it.

I know my little one but all you must do is one day at a time. Just today my little one, that is all I am asking of you.

It has been such an important things for me learn, to do one day at a time with Jesus. It keeps me from being overwhelmed when I feel like I can't keep on walking on this path. It keeps me focused on Jesus. Jesus has asked me to live a life that I can't live in my own strength, where I'm seen as someone I'm not and for the most part, for Pearl to be hidden from view. His purpose in this, in this part of the path, is that I learn to see myself through his eyes and not through the eyes of other people. He has set me free from the lies of the past that told me who I was and in living hidden away from others I have had to go to him over and over again to find out who I am, to rely on what he says about me because I know that the people I'm with every day don't even really see me or know who I am. He has become my truth.

My little one I am helping you to see the truth, the truth of your life and who you are. They are not the same my little one. Who you are is hidden in me. Who you are comes from me for you were created by me my little one. You were created with love and you are loved still. My little one the truth of your life is painful and hard for you to accept but it does not change who you are my little one. You are who I have made you to be. You are delightful and you are lovely and nothing that the enemy has done or will do can ever change that my little one.

It is hard to see myself. I get lost in all that stuff.

That is why you must hold on to me my little one. I am your truth. Everything that you need comes from me. There is nothing that can ever change that my little one. I will show you the truth and I will enable you to accept it. My dearest one I know that for you to do this you have to let go of so much that you thought you were and so much that you hoped to be but my way is so much better my little one. The truth is so much more wonderful than anything that you have believed.

I want to see it Jesus, the truth. I do.

My little one I will help you. I am helping you. My dearest one when you look at yourself you do not see what I see. Your vision is clouded and confused for you have not yet taken hold of the truth though you are beginning to see the glimmers of light that I am showing to you. My dearest one as you begin to see who you are your perceptions will change. I know that the past is painful my little one and that you are afraid of what it will mean for you in the future but I am your future my little one. No matter what has happened in the past I am your future.

Yes. It kind of feels like wearing glasses that make me see things in a different way and I'm not quite sure where I am walking or what I am doing. I suppose I will get used to it.

Yes my little one you will. A shift in perception takes time to adjust to but it will come my little one. Do not be afraid to see the truth.

I am less afraid. Maybe because I know that you are here, holding me and I won't fall but I need your help to see things how you do.

My dearest one I am helping you and I will not stop. My dearest one all that you are is hidden in me. I know that you know this and yet you have not understood it. I will help you to understand it my little one for it will help you to see the truth of who you truly are. My dearest one the horror you feel when you look at the past will fade, the pain and fear will fade and all will be healed in time but who you are will not change my little one. You are already beloved. You are already my child, you are already everything that you will ever need to be. These things will not change my little one.

Yes. I know I am not seeing things from your point of view Jesus, but at least I can see that now.

Yes my little one you are moving forward day by day. I am helping you to see my little one slowly as you are able. Hold on to me, keep on trusting me. My little one you may not see the way that others see, your experience may be completely different to theirs and what is unacceptable to them may be acceptable to you and visa versa but my dearest one it does not matter what others think or how they see you or your life. Often the truth will be hidden from them my little one but it will not be hidden from you for I will reveal it to you and enable you to live in the truth of who you truly are. Not the truth of who the world says you are my little one but the truth of who I say you are.

Yes. I think I see that. A little.

My little one you are delightful to me in every way. As you begin to see the truth of this for yourself you will begin to see yourself differently my little one. You will not feel the way that you do now.

Please hold on to me Jesus because I feel very unsteady. I am willing to see the truth Jesus but it knocks me over every time. I want it to be ok to be me but it still isn't, not for me anyway.

I know my little one. Keep your eyes upon me and listen to my words of truth. They apply to you my little one. You are not exempt because of who you believe you are. You are my child chosen by me. Created in love to be all that I desire my little one. You are qualified for everything that I am longing to give to you.

Chapter 10

The Path of Freedom

Being free means able to make my own choices. Jesus gives all his children free choice, it is his gift to us but so often we use that choice to turn away from him, to do bad and evil things like the people that hurt me did.

Jesus I don't know why darkness is so strong if it is already defeated.

Because my little one the battle is won but it is not yet over. The battle continues my little one even though the end is not in doubt.

Why did you give us choice Jesus?

Because you are my children my little one, it is part of who you are. You are so much more than you know yourself to be. Being my child means that you have choice, that is the way that you are made.

The two go together somehow.

Yes my little one they do.

You couldn't make us in your image if we didn't have choice.

No my little one.

Why weren't you happy just to be you? I mean why did you want to have children when it meant so much pain and suffering for you and for them. I don't understand that.

Suffering is not the evil you believe it to be my little one and many things are accomplished through it.

Pain is not the enemy.

No my little one it isn't.

But there's no pain in heaven so you must want there not to be pain and suffering Jesus.

My little one many things happen that I do not want because things here on the earth, in the life you have here, are broken and do not follow my will. That is not so in heaven my little one where everything is perfect. The suffering that you see around you is because of the choices that have been made against my will and against the things that I wanted for my children. Suffering came with choice my little one for the choices that mankind have made have often been to turn against me. That does not mean my little one that there is no choice in heaven but only that each choice that is made will be for me and not against me. Perfect choices my little one. Choices led by love and not by fear.

Fear is the enemy and where there is perfect love there is no fear and all the choices made will be perfect.

Yes my little one.

I suppose you use the choices that people make, that bring suffering, to draw us back into your perfect love, like you have with me.

Yes my little one that is what I do. Suffering is not an evil my little one, not when I take it and use it to draw you back to me.

But it's not what you want.

No my little one it is not what I want. I do not want my children to suffer my little one I want them to know who they are and who I am. I want them to come home to me.

To the place where there is no suffering.

Yes my little one.

I am still looking forward to heaven Jesus but aren't you going to let me show people who you are, as your Pearl?

Yes my little one I am. When it is time.

And your timing is perfect.

Yes my little one it is.

Jesus gave us all the gift of free choice, but the enemy works hard to take that choice away, to control our choices for us. We never really understood about choices, they were taken from us right from the very start. And even though it seemed like we were choosing...really we weren't. That was something we needed to understand so that Jesus could set us free from the guilt and shame that was holding us, because of the things that we did.

I say that you are innocent my little one and not deserving of any punishment.

I know that you forgive Jesus and I am glad of that but are you saying I don't need forgiveness?

No my little one you do not for the crime was not yours, others are responsible my little one. What you need is freedom from the guilt and the shame and the false belief that it was your fault. It was not your fault my little one. None of it was your fault.

Was it my alters fault?

Some of them played an active role my little one, you were only an onlooker, you took part in the experience, but you did not take part in any choices that were made. Your alters, those that were involved and took an active role, also had little or no choice my little one. You were, as one, conditioned and trained from the very beginning. All of your choices were taken from you. I do not hold any of your alters

95

responsible for the things that they did my little one any more than I do you.

So it wasn't any of our fault?

No my little one it wasn't.

Even if we were old enough to know it was bad?

My little one even a very young child knows that those things are bad. The difference is usually that an older person has more ability to choose their actions. Not so with you or your alters my little one. You never had any choice and so it does not matter whether you were five or fifteen. You were not responsible.

So what do I do Jesus?

Just what you have been doing my little one. Keep seeking my way for you. My dearest one freedom will come and is coming. All you must do is accept the truth my little one that it wasn't your fault.

Yes. Why can't I do it Jesus?

It takes time my little one. It takes time to accept the truth when all of your life you have believed the lie. My dearest one you have spent many years believing in your heart that you are bad, that you deserve to be punished because of the things you did, for you were always aware of them even if you did not remember them. My little one it is a lie, a lie that has controlled you for so long. It is time my little one to accept the truth and let go of the lie so that you can be free and understand the truth of your life and the things that have happened. So that you can find healing and hope and know that it is not wrong for you to have life and love and all the things that you long for.

While I was hidden away on the inside, not knowing I existed, I didn't know I had any choices to make. I didn't have any control over the outside life.

All my choices were taken. Other people made choices and I have to live with them.

Yes my little one you do but not in the way you think. You are not trapped by the choices they made my little one. They have shaped you in many ways, they have hurt you and given you a life you do not want but you are not trapped by them my little one. I am using all of the choices that were made for you and against you, to bring you life and healing and hope and through you to bring those same things to others. My little one you have lived a life that has been for the most part determined by the choices of others and you are still living with some of the results of those choices my little one, but there is a way forward for you, you are not alone. I have restored your ability to

choose my little one and you have chosen me and my way for you. That is good my little one, it is very good. There are many people in this world my little one who believe they have the freedom to choose, but really they do not. Their choices are determined by many things my little one and not many of them are free choices, but you my little one, in all of your struggles and all of your pain have learned how to choose. You have learned what it means to choose my little one and how very precious and how very powerful that is. Do not underestimate this gift my little one. It is a gift even though you have lost so very much to obtain it. Your life is in my hands my little one but

but that was your choice and no one else's. Even though so very much has been taken from you including your ability to choose, I have restored it back to you my little one and will continue to do so as you continue to choose me.

But it wasn't just that I was hidden away, the enemy took all of our choices with lies and deceit. They controlled our choices with fear. That is why Jesus always told us that pain wasn't the enemy, fear was. Fear keeps us from choosing Jesus' way, fear keeps us bound. Fear controls what we do and say. Fear torments us and keeps us from knowing the joy that Jesus has for us.

Holy Spirit.
Yes my little one.
I don't like it when the monsters are waiting for me.
I know my little one but you are able to discern the difference, they did not fool you little one.
No not this time. It is hard to live in the spiritual world Holy Spirit.
It is difficult my little one because the enemy does not want you to see and understand the things of the spirit, he does not want you to have confidence in what you are seeing and hearing but persevere my little one and you will overcome. All you must do is persevere and continue to seek the truth. My little one if you are truly desiring truth, he cannot deceive you.
Is that true?
Yes little one. You must give him permission to deceive you, he cannot do it otherwise.

97

How do I give him permission Holy Spirit?

By believing lies over the truth and by preferring those lies my little one, for whatever reason.

Is that true?

Yes my little one. Even the lies that hurt you are only there because you believed them as truth and gave them permission. My little one for someone who does not know the truth it is easy for them to be deceived for they cannot distinguish between the truth and the lie. Not so with you my little one. You know the truth for the truth dwells within you.

So, I don't know what you are saying Holy Spirit. Is it my fault then that I think, that I believe things that are not true?

Only in as much as you continue to choose to believe them my little one. As soon as you begin to choose to believe the truth the power of the lie begins to weaken and will eventually be broken my little one and the truth will take its rightful place.

So, I don't Holy Spirit because sometimes the truth, it seems like a lie and the lie seems like truth because, it does.

Yes my little one that is so. When you have believed something and all your life it has seemed to be true then for you it takes on the appearance of truth. But that is all that it is, the appearance.

Like when the monsters pretend to be you or Jesus, it seems like you but it's not.

Yes my little one it is the same. The lies disguise themselves as truth and will give you many reasons to believe that they are in fact the truth when they are not my little one. They are lies disguised as truth. The truth is only to be found in us little one. Not what you see or feel or experience, not what life has taught you or what other people say. The truth is only found in us little one and in what we say.

So like the things I believe about me that you say are lies, they are pretending to be truth so that they can hurt me.

Yes little one and they can only stay because you allow them to, because you keep on believing that they are what they say. Like with the monsters, they cannot deceive you once you have seen the truth of who they are little one. They must leave. So it is with the lies.

You make it sound like lies are monsters too.

No little one they are not monsters, but they are from the monsters, sometimes they are attached to the monsters.

Like bindings and they pull them and tighten them and remind me that they are there, they hurt me with them.

Yes little one. But once you start to resist and to believe the truth, or at

least choose to believe the truth, the bindings begin to loosen, and they lose their power over you.

How... but they need to go completely don't they?

Yes little one they do. That is the power of truth in you. The truth will always overcome the lie my little one. As the bindings weaken and the truth takes hold, the hold that lie has on you weakens further and can be stripped away my little one, sometimes it falls away, displaced by the truth but often it has to be removed my little one. Sometimes this takes time if the bindings are strong, sometimes the lies go so deep that it takes much time and healing to drive them out completely my little one but you can be free of them. You can be covered by and saturated with truth.

But I have to start with choosing.

Yes my little one. The truth will not ever take hold while you are choosing to believe the lie.

Why are you telling me this now Holy Spirit?

Because it is time to take another step little one, another step towards the truth. Little one you are constantly besieged by the lies of the enemy. That is not your fault my little one, for they have had so much power over you and bound you in so many lies that have gone so very deep. But now you are beginning to see and to understand little one. You are much more able to choose to believe the truth, even though the lie is still there.

Yes. I see that. Sometimes I know what the truth is, but I don't believe it, like that you love me. Sometimes I believe it a bit but there is a lot of me that doesn't.

Yes my little one there is the beginning of freedom but the lie goes so deep that it will take time to remove it completely.

I have learned too that every time I listen to fear, its hold on me grows stronger, and every time I stand against it, its grip on me loosens. It is only by choosing to trust Jesus over and above the fear that the grip fear has on me has been broken. That is how I have broken free. Not in my own strength but in the strength, Jesus gave me. Over and over he has asked me to choose, often when I least wanted to or felt weakest. It is in those times when we choose to trust, when the fear is greatest, that Jesus can use our choice to break us free of the hold that the enemy has over us. It is a battle. Every choice is a battle but the more we choose to trust, the easier it becomes because the hold that fear has over us becomes less and less. It doesn't mean I don't feel fear, but the fear doesn't control me in the way that it did. It doesn't tell me what to do.

Fear controlled our choices for a long time. We weren't free to make our own choices because of what we believed about ourselves. Shame kept us bound, kept us quiet and hidden. Shame is a kind of fear, a fear of being seen for what we believe we are...bad. It is only the truth of who we are that can set us free from shame.

My little one I know that it is hard for you to see yourself and that you would rather see yourself as Jennifer, but that is not who you are my little one. You are the one we are calling Aj, the one that I love and cherish and adore. You are the one I have chosen my little one. Do not be afraid to let Jennifer go when the time is right. You will be well able in me to do everything that I ask of you. And that is all that you must do my little one.

[I had a picture which isn't easy to describe. It was like a shell being pulled away from soft flesh underneath, I could see the membrane that was joining up the shell and flesh and it was tearing so that the shell could come away from the flesh]

My little one there must be separation between you and Jennifer so that you can be seen more clearly. That is my desire my little one, for you to be seen. Do not fear this my dearest one you will not be despised or rejected. You will be loved, and you will be healed. I am with you protecting you and loving you.

Jesus.

My little one what you are seeing is a combination of brokenness and lies. I will heal the brokenness and strip away the lies so that you can be seen for who you truly are my little one. The wonderful child that I see, the person I created you to be. I know my little one that you feel ashamed, but the shame is not yours. The shame belongs to those who hurt you so badly my little one. There is no shame and no condemnation for you. You are my precious and beloved child. You are being healed and restored, delivered from great darkness my little one. The road to healing is not easy my little one, but this road also leads towards all that I have for you, including myself my little one. It is a road worth travelling even if it is hard and painful. My dearest one I will be your covering. You do not need Jennifer or anyone else to cover your shame. It is already covered my little one, long ago. It is dealt with and now you are mine and free to be everything that I have made you to be.

I'm sorry Jesus I just can't find any words. I understand but it is hurting.

I know my little one but I am holding you and strengthening you. I will help you with everything my little one. Everything that you are is held by me and loved by me. My dearest one though this time is hard and painful what I am doing is so necessary for your healing my little one. It cannot be missed out or avoided. I will help you my little one. I will give you all that you will need. Jennifer will still be with you in your day to day life, to help you in all the ways that you need but you will become more aware of yourself my little one and of all that you are. You will find this painful at first but as I heal you, you will see the change. I am preparing you my little one for the life that is to come. Do not be anxious then that I have forgotten my promises to you for I am bringing them about even now. Everything I am doing is necessary my little one.

I don't want to see myself Jesus. Help me to look at you.

Do not be afraid of what you will see my little one. You are loved just as you are. There is nothing that the enemy has done that makes you less loveable or acceptable. You are precious and beloved no matter what you think you see.

I am afraid. I am afraid of what I will see. I am afraid of the past. I don't understand why I am like this Jesus, not really.

My little one great evil was done to you and though you had many ways of surviving, still you were gravely hurt. My little one I know that you still fear the truth of your life, but I will help you with that also. It is not too much for me to heal or overcome my little one. There is nothing that the enemy can do to steal you away from me.

Why do they keep saying I belong to them?

Because they are liars my little one, but they understand the power of their lies over you. My dearest one I know you do not understand for you are still protecting yourself from the truth. I will reveal it to you in time my little one but for now continue to cling to me and remember that you belong to me. You are my own beloved child and you are safe, and you are secure in my arms. He cannot take you from me my little one and I will never give you up. I will hold you close to my heart all the days of your life my little one. Do not fear him but remember who I am and my great love for you which will never fail.

Knowing the truth in my heart has been so important because it has given me the freedom to choose, to make my own choices which aren't controlled by the lies of the enemy. It has been a battle to choose the truth over the lies, even when I understood there was a choice to be made, which often I didn't to begin with. It took me a long time to see that I had a choice and to see the choices that I was making and what that meant for me. It took a long time for me to see that even though choosing to believe lies was easier for me, it only leads to more pain.

It is the same when it comes to choosing the things I do and say. The things Jesus asks often seems difficult or even impossible, sometimes frightening and painful. It often seems easier to do the things I know aren't what Jesus would want, to follow the path the enemy has for me. They trick me into thinking I'm doing what I want but really, I am doing what they want following the enemy, following the path of death instead of the path of life.

That is right my little one, in following the wishes and desires of the enemy you harm yourself and others but many of our people have yet to truly understand this little one. They see it as a restriction of their right to choose but that is not what it is little one. We never restrict anyone's right to choose we only show them the way to life. Whether they accept it or not is always up to them.

Yes but the enemy fools us doesn't he into thinking it won't hurt or it doesn't matter or that your way isn't good and you don't want good things for us.

Yes little one he does. He will try to persuade you that you can find a better way little one or that our way is too hard or too costly. None of this is true little one. Follow us with all of your heart and you will find life, true life little one not the death life that the enemy gives.

Yes. It is all a big lie what he says.

Yes little one it is but many listen to him little one.

Yes. I listen sometimes. I am sorry.

I know little one but remember this, that our way is the best way. It is the way of hope and of life and of peace. Little one he will try to lead you astray if he can but do not ever listen to him little one.

I need your help Holy Spirit because I can't do that on my own. His lies are, they seem like truth and I get confused.

Yes little one but we will always help you to see and know the truth. Little one you will help many to find their way through the maze of the enemies lies. He spins a web little one and many are caught in it but we will work through you to bring truth to many who like yourself have been caught in his web. You will help them to see the truth my little one and with the truth will come freedom and healing.

Yes. The truth is very important Holy Spirit.

Yes little one the truth is very important.

And it is a lie to think you can do what the enemy wants and not be under his power.

Yes little one that is a lie for as you come into agreement with him, which is what sin is little one, you give him power and influence over you. He will do all he can to make this happen little one for then he can begin to destroy you by your own choices.

But that, I mean he has always had power over me because of the lies and maybe other things I don't understand yet.

Yes little one he has had a great deal of power over you but you are breaking free little one. Choosing us always leads to freedom.

Years ago Jesus gave us a vision of his plans for us, plans to break through the lies of the enemy, to set people free from the things that are holding them. At the time this vision didn't make much sense to us but I have a much better understanding of it now.

June 2007 A vision

I see a cave entrance, which is shaped like the doorway to an old church. I try to enter but there's a barrier of thick, grey, like cobwebs. I break it down and pull it aside. I go into an old church. It feels cold, empty, dark. I see a person approach, they are shrouded in grey. I push the shroud aside. Then I see rows of people sitting in pews. They are grey, faceless, shrouded and unmoving. I move further into the church, but my progress is stopped by many cobwebs. I cut them down. I have many angels with me who also clear the way. We go to the back of the church where the cobwebs are dense. I use my sword to cut through. There I see a spider, bigger than a person, which turns and spins a web back over what was cleared. We cut it down again and advance on the spider. We encircle it, an angel binds it, then with one action we all plunge our swords into the spider and it is gone. We go back to the people who I see are chained to the pews. We cut the chains and drag people out. They are covered in thick, black shrouds, like mourning/funeral clothes, their faces can't be seen. Filled with compassion I pull one off and the person, who still looks stunned and half-asleep is revealed. I put my hands on the person and golden light comes from my hands onto the person. The angels are pouring oil onto the freed people. Light is streaming into the church. There is joy and laughter.

As Jesus has helped me to choose, over and over he has shown me how powerful and important my choices are, how they can mean the difference between being able to follow him on his path or remaining where I am. Still loved and wanted, still Pearl, but no nearer to taking hold of his promises to me. No nearer to being who I am created to be. It is my choice who I become in this life...that has been a scary thing for me to learn.

As I approached the city there were many choices for me to make, so that I could go forward with Jesus, choices to overcome the fear I felt... not just of the choice being made, but of having that choice.

My little one I have not brought you all this way for nothing. I am not cruel my little one.
What are you then, because it is cruel to show me this when I know I can't have it. It isn't mine. I can't have it. Stop it...crying...

Jesus squatted down in front of me and wiped away my tears. I looked up into his face. He looked so kind and full of love.

You are going to have to do something Jesus. He picked me up in his arms.
My little one the city is yours. It is given to you in love. I know my dearest one that you still do not really see or understand but you know that I do not lie. Your journey has brought you to this point and whatever lies ahead you journey with me my little one. I will not leave you.
I just don't want you to promise me things that aren't coming. It looks so close and I am looking for outside changes that aren't coming. They aren't. So what does this mean except that you are showing me something I can't have? I don't want to see. It is too much…crying.
He kissed me and stroked my hair.
It is not too much my little one.
If it is real Jesus and all the things you promised are really coming, you said you would make me able to receive them. Well I think if they did come I would run away.
And that is why you are on this journey my little one because I know how difficult it is for you to receive what I am giving to you, for many reasons. My dearest one will you trust me to lead you one step at a time down towards the city of your promise. Each step is important my little one. Each one requires a choice. And each one will enable you to receive what I have for you.
Are you saying we will take one step at a time and each step is me making some kind of choice. And those choices will help me to receive the promise?

104

Yes my little one that is what I am saying.....My little one for a long time you had no choices to make. All of them were taken from you my little one. Even when you had choices, you chose what you thought would keep you safe. That has been true for all of you my little one and that is not free choice. Free choice is my gift to you and it is only now that you are able to see this and begin choosing for yourself. I know that it is frightening my little one but I will always help you.

I don't know if I want free choices Jesus. I don't know what to do with them.

My little one free choice is a good thing and not a bad one. It enables you to draw closer to me and to follow my plans for you in a far greater way. It is not to be feared my little one.

But it feels a bit like being on my own.

But it is not my little one for I am always with you and will always help you.

It feels scary and overwhelming like I'm not safe. That is silly.

No my little one it is not. I will help you.

So all this time I could have been choosing things that could have helped me, that you wanted me to choose and I have been waiting for you and you have been waiting for me and it is my fault....crying.

No my little one you were not ready. You were not ready to see the truth of your choices my little one and you were not able to take hold of them but now you are my little one. That is a good thing. It means that you are healing and growing stronger.

I like it better when you tell me what to do or I don't have a choice.

I know you do my little one but there is a better way.

Why is it better?

Because it helps you grow my little one. It helps you become who you were made to be. It helps you grow stronger in who you are. My little one it is a different thing to see the choices before you, and to make a choice according to who you want to be, or the direction you want to go in, than it is to simply follow instructions.

Is that being free?

Yes my little one it is.

It doesn't feel safe.

Only because you are not used to it my little one. It is safe because I am with you.

I have been getting it all wrong.

You have been obedient and followed me my little one that is not wrong.

But there is more.

Yes my little one there is.
I don't want to be afraid.
I know my little one.
But I don't know what to do.
You follow me my little one just as you have always done but within that there are many choices that you can make. This is a good thing my little one. Knowing that you have choices is a good thing.
Yes but it is scary.
I know my little one.
We have made choices before like with running and stuff. I don't know why, It just seemed like a good thing to do. Maybe you helped us make that choice because it was important.
Yes my little one I did.
I don't know. I am afraid.
Why my little one?
Because I don't know what you want me to do. It is a bit like you took the stabilizers off my bike.
Because you are ready my little one.
That must be a good thing even if I fall off sometimes.
Yes my little one it is. It means that you can learn to ride properly and you will be able to go places you would not otherwise be able to go.
Yes. I see that. But...you will help me?
Always my little one.

Through all the things that I have been through to take hold of the healing and life that He has for me, Jesus has been restoring my choices. He has shown me how powerful and how important each choice I make is, how my choices can lead to life or they can lead to death. My path has taught me to see and understand the choices I am making, to see them as Jesus sees them. The freedom I have to make these choices has come with the truth... the truth has set me free.

Chapter 11

Freedom to Forgive

Understanding the truth about who Jesus is has set me free to forgive. It has meant I can trust him to bring justice where it is needed, and I don't need to carry that burden for myself. I have forgiven those who hurt me, sometimes many times. Forgiveness is necessary for healing because unless we forgive, we can't surrender the hurt to Jesus so that he can heal it. Sometimes in choosing not to forgive we are clinging on to the hurt and the pain and the anger to somehow justify our need to punish those who hurt us. It can be hard to let go of that.

One of the difficult things about my path has been to stay and keep on living life as Jennifer. It has been difficult and painful for a lot of reasons but one of them is that I see mum regularly. It is hard for me to be with her sometimes, I call her mum but to me she isn't. She doesn't even know who I am, not my name or anything about me. I have forgiven her many times for the things she did when I was a child. I have to keep on forgiving her. Even though there were so many who hurt me she has been the hardest one to forgive, maybe because I still see her or maybe because I still have a need for a mum who loves and cares for me.

I have wanted to escape from Jennifer's life so many times, I have been desperate to escape but Jesus has always asked me to stay. It is his path and this is part of it. There are many reasons for that of course, many things that this part of the path has given and is giving me but part of it is this. Learning to forgive and to keep on forgiving is necessary for me to walk the path Jesus has for me. It will be just as necessary in the future as it is and has been. Jesus has made it clear that many people won't believe my story, will attack me in different ways, try to destroy me. It comes with following him. I understand that but if I can't forgive my enemies I will be lost. I won't be able to follow where he leads. It would destroy my purpose.

So difficult as it is my path has meant spending time with mum, having a relationship with her that is based on love and kindness. That is what Jesus wants it to be even when she is often the last person I want to spend time with. When we first remembered and realized what she had done we fought so hard against it, tried to excuse it, tried to understand it. It tore us apart for a long time trying to find some way to accept it, and then to forgive her. What I learned from that is that the enemy is quick to use any unforgiveness against us. While we wrestled with the truth and the need to forgive, the enemy took full advantage. While I was judging her, I was standing in Jesus place. I can't ever do that. I am not the judge. I trust the one who is and rest in his ability to know and understand the truth.

I remember the thing about mum. We were tormenting ourselves, or maybe it was the enemy who was tormenting us I don't know, with why she did what she did and how could she do it and struggling to believe it but knowing that at least some of it was true and feeling so much pain about it. I don't think I even realized it was something that forgiveness could help, but you took us to that bit in the bible where David has a chance to kill Saul, but he doesn't because it is up to you to judge him and he is going to honor the king, because he was the king. And we knew you were speaking to us and telling us that we had to surrender mum to you and leave you to judge and know what she did and why she did it. And that we needed to love and respect her, because she is our mum no matter what she did. And that should have been really hard to do Jesus, but somehow it wasn't, because we saw and understood that you are God and we are not, and that we could trust you with that. And that was when we forgave her and trusted you with knowing and judging and the pain went and it was so much better. No more tormenting and we have been able to spend time with her and love her and though it has been a bit scary sometimes because I get hurt easy it has been ok and we never felt that same way again. I just want you to save her and love her Jesus. That's forgiveness isn't it?
Yes my little one it is.
And I think forgiveness is you helping me to forgive, that was a gift to me Jesus. Maybe to her I don't know but mostly to me, because it set me free and I think brought healing.
Yes my little one it did. My dearest one holding on to the need to judge and to bring some form of punishment to those who have hurt you is to put yourself in my place. That is never a good thing my little one. It twists your soul and brings pain and torment as you have seen.
But what about, like seeing someone convicted of a crime, that's not wrong is it?
No my little one that is not wrong. The criminal justice system allows for punishment to fit the crime my little one and to bring protection from that person committing the same crime again, but it does not mean that you cannot forgive that person my little one.
No, I see, kind of. But no one will ever be put in jail for what they did to me Jesus.

108

No my little one perhaps not but that does not mean that there is no justice for you my little one.

No. But I am not very sure what that is. Do I need to know there is justice before I can forgive? I suppose, I trust you to bring justice so, maybe yes.

Yes my little one trusting me will always help you to forgive those who hurt you.

I expect there will be a lot more forgiving for me to do.

Yes my little one there will. As we journey together you will discover many more people from the past who will need to be forgiven and there will be those in the present who will hurt you my little one and you will need to forgive them also.

You will help me though Jesus.

Yes my little one I will.

I think you forgive me for all the things I do wrong Jesus and that is a big gift and I am not sure I know how big it is but I think you helping me to forgive those who hurt me, that gift is big too and maybe I see that a bit better.

My little one I will help you to see and understand the true power of forgiveness, both in your life and in the life of others. You are right my little one in saying that it is my gift to you. One of many that must be taken hold of time and time again my little one as you journey with me.

Some people, they don't seem to want your gift Jesus not either part of it. They don't want forgiveness for themselves and they don't want to forgive either. Why is that?

Sometimes it is because they do not fully trust me my little one, sometimes it is because they are unwilling to face the pain of what was done to them, and sometimes my little one it is because they have allowed the enemy to enter their heart and cause it to turn bitter. Bitterness is a terrible thing my little one. It destroys those who have it and has only one cure my little one.

What is that Jesus?

Forgiveness my little one, that is the cure. Forgiveness for their own wrongdoing and forgiveness towards those who have wronged them.

But they have to see that they need help, they need truth first Jesus. Like with everything I suppose.

Yes my little one they do and as with everything it begins with choice my little one, a willingness to see the truth of the condition of their own hearts.

You helped us to do it Jesus, all of those things. They are all hard and painful.

Yes my little one they are, but they are possible...for everyone they are possible.

Everyone Jesus?

Everyone my little one.

That is good news.

Yes my little one it is very good news.

I don't remember forgiving grandad Jesus, maybe it just seemed to happen.

My little one you made a choice in your heart to forgive everyone who hurt you. It is your heart that matters my little one and the choices that you make, the rest follows.

I understand that to follow Jesus means to walk in forgiveness, always and for everyone, no matter what. That isn't easy but it is possible because I understand the truth. The truth about who Jesus is and how he is the only judge this world needs, not me. So I leave it to him. I trust him and I accept his gift, he helps me to forgive those who hurt me. That way I can walk the path he has for me, that is what his path has taught me.

Forgiving those who have hurt me has only been one part of it though. As Jesus has led me forward into the healing he has for me, he has shown me the truth of many things. Often the most difficult truth for me to see is what is in my own heart. My anger towards those who hurt me was hard to face, but to me it seemed wrong that I was angry with Jesus and most of all, that I was angry with daddy God. How can you be angry with someone you believe is perfect? How can that be right? And if I'm wrong to feel that way, how can I accept that I do, how do I forgive someone when I know I am wrong to be angry with them?

My little one the healing that you experienced in the past through your alters was real. It is not gone but you are you my little one and we are bringing a deeper measure of healing, so that there can be no question in your heart whether you are loved and cared for and protected. So that you will know that you have a daddy who loves you and cares for you and has always done so.

I would like to know that, but it doesn't seem true to me Jesus. But then I remember you and all the bad things that happened to you and you didn't seem to think he didn't love you. Even when he turned away from you at the end and you felt like he abandoned you. Can you tell me about that and help me understand?

My little one I knew I had a purpose in this life. My purpose was to show our children just who the father is. They needed to see him in the

flesh my little one, so that they could see and understand who he is and how much he loves them. My little one when I came, I came representing our daddy I was not separate from him. Everything I did, I did with him and for him. My little one everything I went through and all the bad things that happened to me also happened to him. We were not, are not, separate in that way. When I gave myself on the cross, he was also giving himself my little one. When I died, I was showing you how much he was willing to give for you. When I cried out in pain that he had abandoned me, he was also crying out my little one, we are not separate. We are one. My dearest one the things you are struggling with come from a need to blame the one you see as responsible for your pain. He is not responsible my little one. He loves you and never wanted any of those things to happen to you. Do you think I am responsible my little one? We are not separate or different.

I know...and there have been times when we did see you were responsible Jesus because you are in control of everything, because you gave people free will so they could hurt me and because you kept me alive. All of those things. I know that you show me who daddy is, that he is like you. He is good and kind and loves me, but somehow, I am angry with him and blaming him. It doesn't make sense, but it does.

You need to forgive him my little one and let go of the anger you feel. Give it to him my little one so that he can love you and help you through it.

How did you know he loved you when bad things happened? People did bad things to you and he let them.

Because I understood my little one that the bad things did not come from him. I understood that he was with me in them. I understood that he was not separate from me and that he was giving me the strength I needed. I understood that there was a good purpose and a plan, and I trusted him my little one because I know who he is.

I know who you are Jesus...crying...

Yes my little one you do.

How can I be angry with him? What do I do with it?

You give it to him my little one.

But how can I forgive him if it's not his fault?

Forgiveness is letting go of your need to blame him my little one. To accept that he loves you even in the midst of all that happened to you, he loved you. He did not leave you my little one.

I think it is easier to be angry.

Yes my little one it is but it is not better. It keeps you from all that we

have to give to you. Your daddy loves you my little one. It has always been so.

I don't want to keep on being angry, but I am not sure I am seeing in my heart why I shouldn't be. It is all wrong. This world is all wrong…crying….

Yes my little one it is but we are making it right again my dearest one. All that we are doing is to make it right again.

But why let what you made get broken in the first place Jesus? That's what I don't understand. If you made a world and your children, so why let it get broken and smashed? Why would you do that when you could stop it? When you knew it would happen…It's not like you didn't know. Why make me just to see me smashed up into pieces? …crying….

My little one the evil in this world does not come from us. I know this is hard for you to understand, and it is even harder for you to understand why we allow it to continue to hurt and destroy the things and the people we love. But my dearest one there is so much more that you have not seen or understood of our plans for this world and for our children. My little one allowing evil to continue, even with all of the pain and suffering this brings, is making something possible that is so beautiful and so very wonderful, that all of that is worth it my little one. Remember that we are with you, with all of you, with our very creation in all of the pain and suffering my little one. We are not separate from it any more than we are separate from you. My little one we do not spare ourselves the pain and suffering of this world, we are in it working through it to accomplish so much more than you could imagine. Far more than I can explain to you now.

Like you say you will work through my suffering, like your suffering accomplished a wonderful thing to save us.

Yes my little one just like that. I know it is hard to understand my little one, but we are part of everything. We do not distance ourselves from it. My little one when you suffer, we suffer. We are always with you. Just as when I suffered our father suffered. He did not distance himself from it my little one.

But didn't he turn away Jesus? I don't really understand about that.

Only because he had to my little one. When I took on the sins of the world, all the things that are not from him, all the things that are against him, I became everything that he is not my little one. He could not be a part of me at that moment my dearest one. He could not be with me in that. It was my burden my little one and I carried it alone for just one moment my little one. That was long enough.

112

I don't think I exactly understand except I suppose that was more terrible for all of you than anything else.

Yes my little one it was.

I know I am wrong Jesus...it's just I know something in me needs to change.

Then forgive him my little one. Give up your need to blame him for the evil in his world and for what happened to you. He is a good father my little one. He will never abandon you.

Will you help me Jesus?

Yes my little one I will.

I had to choose to forgive daddy God so that I could be free to receive his love for me, a love that I need not just to heal but to be me, the person I truly am. I can't be Pearl Sunshine without knowing I am loved by my daddy God. I need him to be me. Jesus led me, all of us, towards daddy God because he knows we need him. We need him because he is our daddy and we aren't meant to live without him anymore than Jesus could live without him when he was here on earth. Freedom to forgive is a precious gift that means I can have the relationship he always intended for me to have with him.

I also needed to forgive myself. One of the lies that the enemy put in my heart from the very beginning was that I was bad, that it was all my fault and I deserved to be punished just for being me. I had to let go of my need to be punished. I had to forgive myself and my alters so that I could move forward and receive the healing and freedom Jesus had for me.

My little one the issue is not my promises or your understanding. It is not even about faith or hope my little one. It is about what you believe about yourself. You do not believe you deserve to have anything good my little one. You are still punishing yourself.

Why am I doing that?

Because you do not believe that you should have lived whilst others died. Because you are angry and ashamed that they were released come their suffering whilst you were not. You are angry at yourself my little one for being strong enough to survive. My dearest one you are my child, I love you with all that I am. I know my dearest one that you are afraid and that you are still ashamed but my dearest one there is no shame for you. I have taken it all from you my little one. Do not try to hold on to it.

But I shouldn't be alive. It is wrong.....Crying

No my little one it is not wrong. You were chosen to live my little one. It

113

was not your choice but mine. My choice my little one and not yours. You did not choose to let so many others die whilst you lived my little one.

I didn't want to live.

No my little one you didn't. My dearest one forgiving yourself for living whilst others died is one thing. Forgiving yourself for not dying and being strong enough to survive what they did not is another. Both need to be let go of my little one.

They are kind of the same thing Jesus.

One speaks of the suffering of others my little one the other speaks of your own suffering. They go together but they are not the same.

How do I forgive myself then?

By understanding my little one that you had no choice.

Like with the bad things I did.

Yes my little one.

I suppose that is true Jesus. I don't see I had any choice. But maybe the alters did. Like Jennifer, she knew how to be strong and keep safe. All the outside alters, in normal times, they could have died. Could they Jesus?

They chose to keep on living my little one. Together they chose to keep on living.

I suppose if one was going to end it another would make sure they didn't, like it didn't matter. There was never any chance to escape. I could never die. I still can't die. Other people get to die Jesus. They die so easy but not me.

My little one forgiving yourself and your alters for not having died, for making the choice to live, even unconsciously and collectively, will help you to take hold of life my little one and begin to truly live.

But I don't know if I do forgive myself. It would have been better…Crying.

No my little one it only seems so to you now. It would not have been better my little one. Not in any way.

I think my head is very jumbled Jesus about everything.

Yes my little one it is for you are being pulled in different directions. You hate yourself for living but you long to truly live my little one. You believe you should have died and not survived what others did not but you understand that you have a calling and a purpose. There is a reason you survived my little one.

I suppose it is about choice again. Now I've got one.

Yes my little one it is.

To forgive myself and the alters for surviving and not dying so that I can live and fulfil the purposes.

Yes my little one that is your choice.

I don't know if I can do it.

You need only choose my little one. I will help you.....My little one your desire is to follow me.

Yes.

And you understand that everything I have for you is good.

Yes, maybe.

And that everything I ask of you is good.

Yes.

Then choose to follow me into life my little one. Let go of your need to be punished for things that were not your fault. Doing so will bring life to many my little one, not only to yourself.

It wasn't my fault…Crying

No my little one. None of it was your fault. Will you forgive your alters for their part my little one.

For keeping me alive?

Forgive them my little one.

I don't know if I can….Crying.

Was what they did bad my little one. Did they do it to hurt you?

No…No. I forgive them Jesus

And yourself my little one?

Yes…Crying

Little one stepping into life takes courage. You are able my little one as you walk hand in hand with me. I will help you and care for you and give you everything that you need.

Forgiveness is the key to following Jesus through a dark and painful world, which will oppose the kingdom of heaven and those who belong to Him. We can't follow Him without it.

Chapter 12

The Path of Rest

As we have walked with him...Jesus has made clear to all of us that to do the things he was calling us to do, to be the person he made us to be, we needed to be able to trust and depend on him for everything. This has been a long, long journey for each of us and now me. Learning to trust him completely is necessary to surrender completely, to walk in faith and not in fear, to follow where he will lead me. Our need to stay safe and be in control has driven so many of our choices in the past. We have struggled to hand over control to Jesus, because we didn't trust him enough to do it, because we wanted our own way believing the lie that it was safer somehow.

Hi my daddy
This morning I was in daddy's bubbles sitting on Jesus lap. The Holy Spirit was there too. In like a hole in the floor I could see down to where I am walking with Jesus towards the city. Like looking down through the clouds. They said that it was to help me see a different view, and that even while I am walking toward the city I am resting in Daddy's arms.

Hi Jesus and daddy and Holy Spirit,

Hello my dearest child we are all of us with you. My little one you are held and you are loved safe in our arms always. We will not ever let you go. Everything that you are belongs to us. My little one these days are precious, they are preparing you for what is to come. Do not be anxious my little one because you do not yet see the promise. It is there only just ahead of you.

It doesn't seem any closer to me. I know you want me to wait in hope and to rest in you. I am trying.

I know you are my little one.

Why am I here looking down on me there?

Because we want you to understand my little one that you are still resting in our arms surrounded by love, safe and held even as you journey with me towards the city. It is not that you are there and not here my little one you are both there and here. We are with you wherever you are.

Yes. I kind of understand. But why can't I see me up here from down there.

Because my little one as you journey towards the city you are walking with me. Your eyes are upon me my little one. It is not different.

It seems different. I suppose this is the place where I can see different. I don't know it doesn't matter.

Yes my little one it does. Whilst you are here with us you can see many things that would be hidden from you otherwise. We can show you all of the paths that you are on and many other things besides. When you are seeing from the path you are focused on that path my little one. You can see ahead of you but not everything.

So you are letting me see from this place to help me.

Yes my little one to help you.

But aren't I always here. I mean will there be a time when I'm not?

No my little one you are always here with us surrounded by love, safe and held and able to see my little one if you are willing.

Because I can see more from up here.

Yes my little one you can.

Why is this helping me?

My little one the journey before you is not long nor is it in vain. My dearest one you have come such a long way to reach this place. As you see your journey from this viewpoint you are able to see what you cannot see otherwise. We want you to see and to understand and not to be afraid of that.

It is what you said to me before that as I rest in you I can see and

117

understand whatever you want to show to me because it's fear that keeps me from seeing.

Yes my little one it is.

But I am still afraid Jesus, daddy, Holy Spirit. I am still afraid a chasm will open up before my feet and there will be a whole other journey to do to get to the city. I am still afraid it will be too long and too difficult for me and I will give up hope. I am still afraid.

Why are you still afraid my little one?

I can't think of a good reason. I am safe and loved and you are in control. My life belongs to you. I belong to you and whatever you want should be ok. I would like to be happy I suppose and all the things you have promised me. I don't know. Why am I still afraid?

Because you have not yet let go my little one.

What of?

Of your need to be in control my little one, of your need for things to be the way you want them to be, within your understanding of what we have promised you. But your understanding is not complete my little one. It is limited by your viewpoint. You have not seen everything there is to see. You have not understood everything that there is to understand. It is only as you let go my little one that you are able to move freely with my spirit into all that we have for you. Until you do that you will be resisting my little one because you will need him to go this way or that so that your needs and expectations will be met but that is not how it is my little one. He is the one who leads not you. He sees everything. He understands all things. He knows the way my little one and there is nothing to fear from it.

I am sorry Holy Spirit.

I know my dearest child but will you take my hand and allow me to lead you forward. Will you listen to everything I say no matter what it is? Will you allow me to show you the way ahead, to help you my little one and not to harm you.

One hand in yours and one hand in Jesus hand?

Yes my little one that way you will walk confidently into all that we have for you no matter what comes against you. No matter what you see or don't see.

Because you see for me.

Yes my little one we do.

So being here with you I see better and that is to help me. And walking towards the city you hold my hands and lead me because you can always see everything and you know the way.

Yes my little one.

And what about outside life? I know it's not different but it seems it sometimes. And you know how that is…crying.

Yes my little one we do and we are there with you also. It is not different my little one.

It is because I still don't want to be here and even if I see and understand my journey better...crying.

My little one we have brought you here to give you hope because there is more before you than you have yet seen. Right now you are walking towards that place my little one. You have not yet reached it. The journey is hard and seems endless to you but it is not. There is an ending my little one and it is for the sake of all that we are giving to you that we are asking you to take this journey with us. I know my dearest one that you just want to be there, you want this part of the journey to be over for you. We understand my little one but we ask you to persevere a little longer for the sake of all that is to come. We have many things that we will ask of you as you walk with us my little one. Many things you have not yet seen. All of it is to help you. All of it is to prepare you. Just because you do not yet see those things does not mean that they are bad or difficult my little one. You do not need to be afraid of them. We are not hiding them from your view because we are unkind but only because we want you to see and accept that you are moving towards the city hand in hand with us and that you do not need to be afraid, not of anything.

I don't know what you want me to say. All I am hearing is that the journey goes on and somehow being able to see the city isn't helping me much.

Will you let go my little one?

I know there isn't much point me holding on. I'm not in control. I can never be in control.

No my little one not in the way you want but that is a good thing my little one.

I know. How do I do it?

I found myself back on the ground in front of the city. I was holding Jesus hand and the Holy Spirit was there too holding out his hand.

Simply take my hand my little one.

I took his hand but crumpled up crying but they both pulled me to my feet.

My dearest child we are leading you forward into the life we have for you. The journey may not be what you expect or even what you want it to be but it will be better by far than anything you have imagined. Come my little one let us walk forward together. We have a journey to

complete and much to accomplish before we reach the city.
I have the best traveling companions…crying.
Yes my little one you do.

The more I have been able to trust the more I have been able to surrender control and to let go of my need to know or for things to be the way I think they should be, within my own understanding of what Jesus has said. Jesus has led me step by step deeper and deeper into a trust that has helped me to surrender to his will over mine. To give him access to my heart, to give it to him, completely. It has taken a long time and has meant making a lot of difficult choices, facing the fear that was holding me, choosing the truth over the lies. Over and over and over again.

It has been especially difficult when things didn't happen the way I thought they would. I spent a lot of time talking to Jesus about the future and his plans but often it didn't look anything like I imagined, the path would take a sudden turn and I would feel confused and afraid. And disappointed, so often I was disappointed because things didn't seem to be the way I thought Jesus said they would be.

When it finally seemed like we could see an end to the healing, when we started to think maybe the promise was close now, all our hopes came crashing down. Jesus showed us a whole new part of the inside world that we didn't even know existed, It meant more alters, more healing. It meant the end that we thought we saw had vanished along with our hope.

How do I keep on trusting you Jesus when nothing you say happens and all that does happen is more stuff and I know the things you promised can't ever happen so why do I keep on trusting you…..Crying.
My little one my dearest little one listen to what I will say to you. I have not ever lied to you. Sometimes you have not understood my full meaning but that does not mean that I have lied or misled you in any way.
But you know what is in my mind. You know what I think and believe and you don't tell me any different. You don't tell me straight. You aren't honest with me. Not lying isn't the same as being honest.
My little one I told you many times that your healing would continue for many years to come.
Yes but that is a bit different. I thought you meant a different kind of healing.
I know my little one and that is so. You need different kinds of healing
120

my little one all of which will be given to you but I did not ever say that the inside healing was finished my little one.

You didn't say there was all this stuff to do either how can I trust you when I never know if what I'm believing is true. I have to depend on you for everything and if you don't tell me nobody will. I can't believe what you say because it never turns out to be what I think. So what is the point of telling me when you know I don't understand? If I can't trust you then there is nothing and nobody. Why should I believe anything you say? Why do you even talk to me? It's been the same thing over and over and over but I don't have anywhere else to go. I don't even have anyone else to talk to. I rely on you for everything so you can do anything you want and I just have to take it. Is that it? Is that who you are?

> *I seemed to be sitting on the floor. Jesus was standing on one side and the Holy Spirit on the other. In front of me were a few steps up to what I knew was daddy's throne. I was dressed in my daisy dress and my shoes of hope and my crown but I was crumpled up and crying. Everything else was white.*

My little one you are loved far more deeply than you will ever know. There are many things you do not understand my little one. You mistrust what you do not understand but understanding in itself is not knowledge my little one. There is something far deeper that we are longing to give to you. If we were to explain everything to you, tell you all of our plans and everything that must happen, all the how's and the when's and the whys it would not help you my little one. That is not what you need. What you need is to learn to trust. When your trust has been broken so many times it is hard for you to take hold of the love that is given to you my little one but trust is necessary. Restoring trust takes time my little one and it will require much courage and tenacity from you. That is because restoring your trust in us is the basis for everything my little one. If we do not tell you everything it is not because we are unkind nor is it because we are dishonest it is because we are helping you to find that trust which has been lost, to mend that which has been broken and to restore everything back to you that has been taken. That is our desire for you my little one. We do not always correct your thinking or tell you everything that it is in our hearts to do but we ask you to choose to trust in spite of that. We know that it is hard my little one. We know that it requires you to take many steps of faith that you do not want to take but my dearest one our way leads to life and not to death. Do not be afraid to keep on following. Do not be afraid to trust even when you do not understand. Do not be afraid of who we are my little one. We are good in every way and will never harm you. Everything we do is to help you my little one even when you do not understand that to be true. Everything that we have promised you will come just as we have said it would. That is true whether you understand it or not, whether you believe it or not my little one. Our promises are real and true.

I still don't understand and I get so tired of all the disappointments and I wonder why all the nice things never come…..Crying.

It is not because we do not love you my little one but because we know who you can be.

I don't want to be that person.

Yes my little one you do. Little one you belong with us. You belong to us. That is a good thing my little one. We are taking you forward in our strength and our love and we will never leave you or forsake you. Do not give up my little one. There is nothing to fear from anything that is ahead of you nor is there anything to fear from the past. We are with you my little one.

Then daddy spoke.

My child there is nothing ahead of you that we have not seen. Nothing that we do not know. My dearest child you are precious and you are loved and everything in the kingdom belongs to you. There is nothing more that we can give to you but we can help you to take hold of that which is given. So few of our children ever truly receive all the things that belong to them. We know the way is hard but the reward is great. Do not be afraid to continue. Do not be afraid of us.

I am afraid. I'm afraid if I come to you I will believe you and then you will keep on tricking me. I can't live without you. I don't want to be hurt any more. I don't want to be hurt any more…..Crying.

We will not hurt you my little one. We will not ever hurt you. We will not leave you my little one.

It has often seemed endless to me and like I was getting nowhere but all the time Jesus has been leading us forward, all the time he has been healing us and setting free, all the time he has been using all of our choices, all of our waiting and all of the disappointments to help us surrender to him in everything, to trust him in everything and most of all to find rest in who he is.

When I had to get a job and go out to work, I was so confused and afraid. I was confused because I had thought Jesus has said I wouldn't have to get a job and I was afraid because I didn't understand. I didn't understand how it was possible for me to have a job and be out there the grownup world. I didn't understand why Jesus would allow it or want me to because he made me a little girl, why did I have to be a grown up. I was afraid because I thought maybe the promise wasn't real and this was going to be my life now, forever. But Jesus wanted to use this confusing and impossible situation to show me how to trust and depend on him completely for everything, to rest in who he is and to know that it doesn't depend on me. I'm not the one who needs to be in control because he is in control and he is always working for my good and will help me in every moment with everything I face. I learned it because I had to. I had to depend on him there was no other way of being able to do the things I needed to or to be the person I had to be.

My little one as you face all the challenges this life brings you, you are learning how to trust and depend on me. Such trust and dependence is necessary my little one and must be complete if you are to do everything that I will ask of you. My little one I know that it is hard for you to see and understand these things right now for much is still hidden from you and you are tired my little one and in need of much rest.

Well why are you asking me to do so much tiring work if you want me to rest.....Crying.

Because it is my rest that you need my little one. I know that you are tired because of all the things that you need to do but it is my rest that you need most of all my little one. It is my strength that you need above your own. It is my sight that you need more than anything you see and understand. It is these things I am longing to give to you my little one.

By showing me how much I need them.

In part my little one. As you cling to me and trust me to give to you all the things that you need I am able to give you so much more than you are asking for.

Like blessed are those who hunger and thirst.

Yes my little one just like that.

So you have put me in a place where I so desperately need you so that you can give me everything you want to.....Crying.

That is part of it my little one. I am using your great need to give you many things that you will need in the future. My dearest one the first thing you need to receive is my rest. That is like a foundation my little one for until you are able to fully rest in me everything else will remain

difficult.

Tell me about your rest.

Trust and dependence my little one. When you are able to fully trust and depend on me for everything then you will receive my rest.

So as I do that through this time because it is so awful you can give me your rest. So I need to trust and depend on you and not doubt or give in to fear but remember who you are and that you love me and I am safe in your arms always no matter what is happening or how things look to me.

Yes my little one.

Trust and dependence then.

Yes my little one.

Please help me then Jesus. This is not fun….Crying

I know it isn't my little one but as you cling to me and trust me to give you everything you need you are able to receive all that I have for you. It is a good thing my little one even if it is difficult.

Well if you aren't faithful and true everything is lost Jesus. So I am going to trust you. You are strong enough to hold me up and keep me going….Crying.

Yes my little one I am.

Like when I am weak then I am strong.

Yes my little one because it is then that I can give you my strength in greater measure. You are learning and growing my little one and as you do you are able to receive so much more. Do not be discouraged my little one. I am so very proud of you. My little one you are my dearly beloved child and nothing will ever change that. Pearl Sunshine is who you are and who I am making you to be. You have not yet seen or understood who that is my little one. Do not give up on her just yet.

It has taken me a long time to really understand what rest is. Rest is complete dependence, rest is total trust. Rest is not needing to be in control but recognizing that Jesus is always in control. Rest is found in knowing who God is, that he is good, always. That he is working for me, always, that he is with me, always. Rest is only possible when I know who he is. Rest isn't dependent on the circumstances I find myself in but only on trusting in the character of God.

Resting does not mean my little one that you are doing nothing. It is about knowing where you are my little one. Safe in my arms, hidden in our father's heart. Resting in his love for you knowing that I will make all things possible for you no matter where you are or what you are doing.

So...but won't I always be resting?

Yes my little one that is our desire, that you should always be resting.
Because everything I do and am will come out of this place of rest.
Yes my little one.
Because when I know that I am safe and held and hidden and loved, that I am here, then I won't be afraid and I can do anything and go anywhere because I know that I am always here with you and that this eternal reality is the one that lasts, the most important one that will never change no matter what else is changing.
Yes my little one.
And that is what you want me to learn deep down in my heart.
Yes my little one it is.
And then I will be unshakable like you said I would be.
Yes my little one you will.
Ok. Help me learn then Jesus.

Rest is necessary to be able to follow with a heart that is unshaken by the things that come against me, to persevere in the face of the impossible, to endure through great trials and hardships and to overcome when hope seems lost. Jesus has spent a lot of time teaching me how to rest.

Jesus began teaching us about his rest in the simplest of ways. It began with his rocking chair. He would take Aj into his arms and sit with her in his rocking chair, talking to her, to all of us. comforting us, helping us to know that we are safe and loved and that we can trust him with who we are.

It has been difficult because to begin with it was hard to understand that it didn't depend on us, on our ability or our strength or anything else. We struggled and strained and often felt like we weren't good enough. We got afraid because we didn't think we could do the things Jesus asked or walk the path he had for us. We were afraid because we knew we didn't have what it takes but Jesus wanted me to learn that it depends on him and not me. It's his strength and his courage that will enable me to keep going, not my own. He is everything I need.

He took me to a green grassy place where there was one flower growing. We sat down beside it.
My little one do not afraid of anything that I will show to you. My little one you are to us a flower. A flower that is opened and blooming my little one.
I don't feel very blooming....Crying...I feel very wilting.

But you are not my little one. Look and tell me what you see.
I see a single pink flower on a long stalk waving in the wind.
Yes my little one and what else.
It is pointing towards the sun. Like it is trying to catch all the rays or maybe reach up to it.
Yes my little one but the flower does not need to reach up for the rays of the sun will always come down to touch it. There is no need for straining my little one.
Is that what I'm doing?
Yes my little one you are blaming yourself for what you do not feel and what you do not see.
Well it must be my fault. I know I am all wrong inside…Crying.
No my little one it is not your fault. It is not your fault. My little one there are many things in your heart that need to be healed, things that keep you from us but they are not your fault my little one. Your heart is towards us just as this flower is turned towards the sun. The flower is not trying to get away. It is not hiding. It does not want to be in the darkness.
No….Crying.
My little one you cannot heal yourself or make yourself do anything that you are not able to. All you must do is come to us and trust us. We know the way my little one. We know everything that you need.

Trust and obedience go together. As I struggled to make the choice over and over again to be obedient, to choose his way over mine in the face of everything I felt it was costing me, I was choosing to surrender to his will for me. I was giving him control over my life. I was learning to rest. I was learning how to be content to follow no matter where my path leads because I trust the one who is leading me.

Holy Spirit?
Watch closely little one what do you see happening?
I think the light makes a path but a very short one Holy Spirit so that the path is only one or two steps in front of me and then it is dark again.
Yes little one what do you think that means?
I think maybe I am thinking about the light of your word is a lamp unto my feet. Your revelation, the light of your revelation Holy Spirit, it lights up the path in front of me but not very far. Just far enough so I can take the next step.
Yes little one that is exactly right. My little one everything that is here is here for a purpose and I will use it to show you many things.

I am wondering why the light is only one or two steps ahead but I think that is, I don't know, it is so that we will stay close to you isn't it?

Yes little one it is. Tell me what your thought was little one.

Well, I was thinking about walking in the spirit and how you walk with us, and how it is you lighting the way and I thought about you being light and shiny and all of that, so I was thinking maybe the light is you, because you are with me and in me, so if that is right...we can't see that path if we aren't walking with you, because you are the one who is lighting it up, maybe that is obvious Holy Spirit.

Yes little one it ought to be but for many of our people it is not. They think they can find the path without me little one, they think they do not need to walk closely with me but can walk on their own and find the right path. It is not so little one. Only those who walk closely with me will find the path that I have for them, for only then will they be able to see it.

Waiting has been such a big part of my journey with him. I have wanted him to go fast, to get through the healing, to reach the promise. I never wanted to wait. But waiting has been necessary for me to take hold of the things he has wanted to give to me. It has helped me learn how to rest and to trust in him to do the work, to learn that it doesn't depend on what I can do but only on what he can do. Jesus tells me he has purpose in the waiting, just like he has purpose in everything. The waiting makes me stronger.

Do you not know? Have you not heard?
The lord is the everlasting God, the creator
of the ends of the earth. He will not grow tired
or weary, and his understanding no one can fathom.
He gives strength to the weary and increases the
power of the weak. Even youths grow tired and
weary, and young men stumble and fall but those
who hope in the lord will renew their strength.
They will soar on wings like eagles, they will run
and not grow weary, they will walk and not be faint.
Isaiah 40:28-31

When I was reminded of these verses, I realized that hoping and waiting go together. If you don't have to wait you don't need to hope. Hope is what makes waiting possible. If you don't have hope, then you aren't going to wait. As I have waited, I have had to hold on to hope. Holding on is what makes me stronger.

Jesus says that holding on to hope is a bit like holding on to the string of a balloon that will carry you up and over all the obstacles that are in your way, that will take you forward towards the thing you are hoping and waiting for. I have let go of the balloon many times and crashed back down to earth, not able to move until Jesus has picked me up and given me back my balloon.

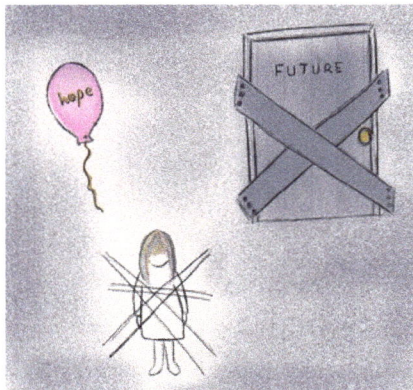

My little one hope is just that. It keeps you moving forward. I know you believe my little one that hope is like a balloon that lifts you off the ground and then drops you. That you cannot rely on it to carry you forward but that is not so my little one. The hope I give to you will carry you forward if you do not let go of it.
So the balloon isn't bursting, I'm just letting go and falling.
Yes my little one you are.
I guess sometimes I let it drag me along the ground, which isn't fun, but you want to lift me up and carry me, let the wind catch me and carry me.
Yes my little one I do.
I suppose it takes courage to hold on to something and let it carry me far off the ground.
What are you holding on to my little one?
Hope, you.
Yes my little one.
And I already have the courage I need to take hold of the hope you've given me and to let it lift me up and carry me forward. To trust in the hope you've given me, that it won't burst and let me fall to the ground and die because that is what I'm afraid of, because it seems like that's what keeps on happening, but all that's happening is I get a little way off the ground and then let go...but you want me to trust it completely so that I can fly high and be carried by it.

Yes my little one I do.
I don't like it. I feel like we've done this so many times before.
But you are stronger now and more able to hold on to what is given to you.
I suppose I can keep arguing and keep my feet on the ground or I can trust you to keep me safe and take hold of the balloon.
You are able my little one if you are willing.

It is scary to go high, to soar on wings like eagles, because there is always the fear that the balloon is going to burst, and I will fall. But Jesus is my hope of course and he isn't going to disappear or fail in any way. It is safe to hope in him and to let hope carry me forward.

I have held on...mostly, and I have grown stronger. On the outside I have grown more confident in Jesus and his ability to do and to be everything I need. It isn't what I want. I don't want to live as grownup Jennifer, going out to work and doing all the other things that go with being an adult. But I can do it because Jesus is with me helping me. This gives me confidence when he tells me about the future. It gives me confidence that no matter how daunting or impossible or even crazy it sounds, I will be able to do it. I will be able to be the person he made me to be, even though I'm still not very sure what that will be like. I have grown stronger in the waiting and the hoping.

For I can do everything through Christ, who gives me strength.
Phil 4:13 NLT

He has used all the disappointments that have come, all the tricks of the enemy, all the mistakes we have made, to help us to surrender our will to his. To learn that his way is always better. That to be in control is not my safe place. Jesus is my safe place and only by surrendering control to him can I ever really be safe. It's not possible to rest unless I know that I'm safe. It's not possible to rest unless I know that I am held and loved at all times. It's not possible to rest unless I know that Jesus is always in control, and that he is always working for me and never against me. Jesus promised to make me unshakeable. I didn't understand what that meant except I supposed it meant I wouldn't be afraid. But it means most of all that I am able to rest in who Jesus is. I don't trust in my own understanding. I don't trust in what I see or know or feel. I trust in who he is. That never changes. The truth of who he is remains no matter what happens. Resting in him is what makes me unshakable.

You will minister from a place of rest my little one, because the needs that you will see will be so very great. You will not be overwhelmed by them as you rest in us but will be able to give us away without fear, knowing and understanding who we are in you and that we are able to do all things, no matter how great the need or how deep the darkness. My dearest one you have learned many things in your journey with us. You have stayed faithful through many trials and you have learned how to draw your strength and everything you need from us. This will continue my little one. It will not every stop for everything you need will come from us. You are our child. You minister from who we are in you my little one. We have more to teach you about these things as you walk with us toward the city. My dearest little one as you become more and more filled with us you will be able to give us away to those in need. That is because of who we are in you my little one. It is because of what we give to you for others. Do not be anxious about what you will say or do for all of those things will be given to you as you have need of them. You need only rest in who we are.

Chapter 13

The Path of Life

Jesus says that he is the way the truth and the life. He is the way, he makes the way for us, he makes the path that we walk with him. He is the truth, all truth is found in him and through him. And he is the life. Our life is found in him and through him. Life is everything that is found in Jesus, everything that he is. It is love and hope and joy. It is peace and purpose. Our life isn't just for here on this earth, but it is eternal. It goes way beyond anything we can experience here on this earth. Choosing life means choosing Jesus, everything that he is, everything that we are and everything he has for us. It means choosing his way, the path of life that leads us closer to him and all that he is.

I have spent most of my life wanting to die, to escape from the life I was living. The pain and the fear and the things I believed about myself meant that more than anything I have wanted to escape from this life, to not be.

I have been in trouble Jesus. Maybe I still am. I want to escape so much and I can only think of one way to do it.

My little one even though this time is hard and there are many things you do not understand I am with you. You do not need to escape my little one this place is giving you life which is my great desire for you.

How is it giving me life Jesus?

What is life my little one?

I'm not very sure. I know you are life but I don't know what that means.

My little one what the enemy desires to give to you is death, which is separation from all that I am. He does this by telling you lies about the future, about the past and about who I am and who you are. He desires death for you my little one because he wants to take you from me but he cannot do it, not in the eternal sense because you already belong to me. You cannot be taken from me but he can keep you from living out your purpose here on the earth. He can keep you from following me my little one. My way leads to life, to all that I am, so that you can receive me deep in your heart, so that we can live and breathe and move as one. That is life my little one. That is who I am. That is what I want to give to you and what the enemy of your soul does not want you to receive.

When I die I will be full of you Jesus and then I will be fully alive.

Yes my little one you will but there is much that you can receive before that time. You can draw so close to me that you overflow with who I am my little one.

I am thinking about Peter and how his shadow healed people, it wasn't his shadow was it though Jesus it was you, flowing out through him kind of like, I don't know he was leaking you everywhere and people got healed.

Yes my little one like that.

And you want that for me.

I want that for all my children my little one.

And that is life, to give away to others like Peter did.

Yes my little one it is.

So how is this time giving me life Jesus? Mostly I feel like it is killing me. But then you do say I have to die before I can live, or something like that.

Yes my little one it is only as you give up everything that you are to me that I can fill you with who I am.

Like I open up my heart completely and I don't keep anything for myself.

Yes my little one.

I don't know Jesus. I think I am not doing well. Me wanting to run away and die, that is me saying I am going to have what I want because what you want is too hard and too painful and I can't do it….Crying.

Yes my little one it is.

Or maybe because I don't think you keep your promises and I don't trust you.

Which do you think my little one?

Mostly the first, mostly…..Crying

And do I ever ask anything of you that is too hard for you my little one?

It all feels too hard Jesus and I don't want to do it and I'm tired, but I know I can do it. I can. I just don't want to, not anymore.

Why my little one?

I don't know maybe it is about control again. Maybe I'm not dying like you say so you can fill me with your life.

And what is it you want my little one? To die as the enemy desires or to be filled with my life, to become who you were created to be, to live out your purpose on this earth, to love me and serve me and do all that I have told you of. What is it you want my little one?

You know what I want Jesus but I lose hope of it. I think I can't do it. It is too hard…..Crying.

But it isn't too hard my little one, not when you have me. What will you

choose my little one? Will you choose my life for you and for others or will you choose death as the enemy desires.

I choose you Jesus always and forever but I don't know how to give it all to you and stop trying to take back control. I don't think I'm brave enough or strong enough…..Crying.

Do you think that I know you my little one?

Yes Jesus. Better than I do.

And do you think I know the way for you to receive everything I have for you, which is my life my little one in all its fullness?

Yes. I'm just not sure I'm willing because it is so hard.

I know it is my little one but you know that I am with you and will help you.

Yes. I'm sorry I fight you and listen to lies when you only want to give me good things. I am having a lot of trouble with your way Jesus……Crying.

I know my little one but you have not let go of me, you have not stopped trusting me even in the midst of all your struggles. I am holding you my little one and you are safe and you are loved. There is nothing to fear from the path I have for you my little one. It is good in every way.

I know it is about following you Jesus and not about getting what I want. It is so hard to be here year after year with all the things that means for me. I know you know. I know you are with me. I don't know how to do it Jesus…..Crying.

But I will show you my little one. As you cling to me and depend on me for everything I will show you.

Jesus has asked all of us, over and over to choose life, his life, over the death that the enemy wanted to give to us. He has had to hold on to us when we weren't strong enough to choose it. He has had to help us choose it over and over again when to us life seemed to offer nothing but suffering, and when we believed that it was just a way to make the suffering last longer. It has taken us a lot of time to learn what life, true life is. Jesus says that his way leads to life, that his is the path of life because it leads to him and he is life. That to choose him is to choose life, his life means freedom from all the things that will keep me from him and from everything he has for me. We have found it hard to keep choosing life when really…we wanted to die.

Do you want to be well my little one?

Yes Jesus I do.

Listen to the truth then my little one. Do not listen to lies. They bring

only death.

Yes but so often I want to die.

Choose life my little one. Choose me.

Maybe, sometimes the life you've given me, it seems not worth living Jesus.

My life has purpose my little one. Always.

I just don't think I can do it…..Crying.

My little one all the time you have been following me have I ever asked anything of you that you could not do?

No. Even if I thought so I always did it.

Yes my little one you are living out of my strength and not your own. You are able to do all things in and through me.

I know I have been messing up. I know I have been listening to lies.

Do you want to be well my little one? Do you want to follow me into everything I have for you? Do you want to love those I give to you and help them to know they are loved by me? Do you want to enter the city with me knowing who you are and who I am and not being afraid of that? Do you want to be well my little one?

Are you my Jesus? Show me who you are.

Take my hand my little one.

I was expecting to see Jesus and take his hand but I saw something else instead. I saw my hand holding the hand of a skeleton wearing a black robe. I knew it was death. At first I was scared I was talking to the enemy but then I realized what Jesus was showing me. That I was holding the hand of death, that is what I have been choosing and why I have been in so much trouble.

You need to let go of your desire for death my little one. Until you do that you cannot take hold of the life I am giving to you. Whilst you have one hand holding on to death I cannot lead you forward into the city. Let go my little one. Let go and trust me fully with all that you are.

I don't know how Jesus. Is that really what I'm doing?...Crying.

Yes my little one it is. It is your way of feeling safe and in control my little one but it is really controlling you. You are not safe in his hands my little one but only in mine.

Like I'm hedging my bets if you let me down….Crying.

Yes my little one but I will not fail you. Not ever.

I know I have been in a battle. I know I have been choosing death because it seems easier. Your way is so hard.

But I am with you in it my little one. Always.

Can I take your hand Jesus? Please….Crying.

Yes my little one but in order to take it you must first

let go of death's hand.

Jesus held out his hand but he was just out of reach. Death was still holding on to me. I had to let go to reach Jesus. So I pulled my hand out of death's and jumped into Jesus arms. Death crumbled into dust.

My little one you are my child, my dearly beloved child. I will help you with everything my little one. You have chosen life. Do not desire anything else. Do not listen to lies. Do not look to the darkness but only the light. You are safe in my arms my little one. You are ready for all that is to come. You are able to follow me even into the city if you are willing. Are you willing my little one?

Yes Jesus. I am willing.

My little one the path before you is clear. You are able to walk it with me. Trust is necessary my little one but it is not too much for you. You have everything you need.

Am I going to make it?

Yes my little one you are going to make it.

In the end it is a choice, one that we must all make and keep on making. The enemy will try to lead us down a path of destruction, a path that leads to death. Often it looks like the easier path, often the path that leads to life looks too painful and difficult. That is why the bible talks about the narrow path that leads to life and the broad path that leads to destruction.

> "Enter through the narrow gate.
> For wide is the gate and broad is the road
> that leads to destruction, and many enter
> through it. But small is the gate and narrow
> the road that leads to life, and only a few find it.
> Matthew 7:13-14 NIV

Jesus wants me to choose life, he wants to fill me with his life, with who he is, so that I can give it away to others. The path he has led me on has been so hard that I have often wanted to give up, to choose death, because it would mean an end to the struggle and the pain. But the difficulty of the path has meant that I have had many, many opportunities to choose life, many times when the choice was so very clear before me in a way that it wouldn't have been if the path had been easier, if the struggle has been less intense.

Were you very lonely?...crying.

At times my little one but I learned how to be with my father in such a way that all the loneliness I felt was held by him, I drew my strength from him my little one and my comfort also for the road I travelled was not an easy one.

No I don't expect any of it was easy.

No my little one it wasn't but I was able because my father made me able, he gave me everything I needed. It did not come from anyone else my little one. Even though I was surrounded by many people, even though there were many who loved me, it was not from them that I drew my strength it was always and only from my father. My dearest one you will have many friends and you will know what it is to be truly loved for who you are but everything that you need to walk through this life and fulfill the purpose that we have for you will come from us. There are many who will help you and comfort you my little one and many who will love you but your need for these things will be met by us and not by them. They are there for you my little one but they cannot ever fill the need that you have which can only be filled by us. Do not hope for it my little one, do not desire it. Look to us for everything that you need my little one.

I don't know if I understand Jesus. Why do you ask us to love people if you are the one they need?

Because in loving them you can show them who I am. In loving them you can give to them the love that I have for them. My little one not

136

many are able to come directly to us and receive from us in the way that you are. They have not travelled the road that you have my little one. They have been unwilling or afraid or unable for many reasons but I will ask you to reach out to them with our love for them my little one so that they can be healed and restored not only in themselves but in their relationship with us.

I am sorry Jesus. Crying.

I know my little one I understand. The road that you are walking is a hard one my little one but in doing so you are learning to draw upon us for everything that you need. That is not so that you cannot or will not receive from others my little one but only so that your source is my father, which is as it should be for everyone my little one. Other people were never meant to fill your need for us, but often that is the way it is my little one. When you have truly learned to draw upon us for everything that you need then you will be able to give without measure just as I did my little one. You cannot do it otherwise. My dearest one we are doing so much more than you know and making you able in so many ways that you have not yet understood. My dearest one as you learn to trust and depend on us for everything, it is then that we can truly fill you and transform you and flow through you to a hurting and dying world. There is a cost my little one, there is always a cost but it is worth it my little one. Hold on to me and trust me just as you have done. I will not leave you my little one and I will fulfill your every need in time. I know the way that I have for you my little one and it is good even if it is hard, it is good.

Choosing life over and over has meant that Jesus could draw me closer, to give me more, more of himself than I would have chosen to accept without the pain and the struggle of the path. He has worked through it all to open up new parts of my heart so that he can bring life, his life to those parts of me that were so wounded they were barely alive. Everything the enemy brought against me to destroy me he has used to bring me life.

My little one, all my promises were made especially for you. Because of who you are, who I made you to be my little one. The enemy has tried to destroy you so many times but I have not allowed him to. Instead I have taken everything he has done and everything he is doing, and I am using it to make you able to follow wherever I will lead you to be who you were created to be, to do the very things that the enemy does not

137

want you to do. My little one the reality of this world is hidden in who I am. You cannot see it apart from me. When you look at your life without first seeing me all you see is meaningless and confusion. But I am neither of those things my little one. Your life is not meaningless and whilst you are following me the confusion in your heart will not keep you from all that I have promised you. My dearest little one I am not cruel or unkind. I know that I am asking much of you but much is being given in return my little one. You can never out give me. Trust me. Hold on to me and do not give up on the hope I have given you. It is real just as I am real. It will not fail you.

I have often wondered what he meant by the promise of the abundant life. It has been so difficult to see anything that I would recognize as that in my life. But what I have learned is that it is a process, often slow and painful, to bring life where there has been only death. He wouldn't do it all at once. I couldn't have accepted what he was wanting to give to me all at once, because my heart was too broken. It had to be gradual. So, it is a promise, a promise that is being fulfilled as I am able to take hold of it. It has taken time, it is still taking time as Jesus heals me, and fills me over and over again, making me more and more his, drawing me closer and making me one with him.

Chapter 14

Journey into the Heart of Love

What is love? That was and sometimes still is a question that we have asked over and over in many ways. It was hard for us to take hold of any love that was given to us, we didn't understand it or trust it. We found it confusing. It was so very hard for all of us to accept that anyone could or would ever love us, we didn't even know what it meant. Did it even mean anything? But love is what has brought me back to life. Love is what has healed me and set me free. Love is what has given me hope and the strength to continue on a journey that a lot of time I wasn't even sure I wanted to take. Love is what has restored my heart, making it new so that it is able to receive what it needs the most, which is more of Jesus. To know that I am wanted for who I am, that I am special, cherished, important. To know that I am safe and protected and held at all times, that I will never be abandoned. That I can totally trust and depend on Jesus to be who he says that he is, to do what he says he will do, that he is good at all times and always working for me and never against me, that all that he wants for me are good things. All of these things and more are found in his love. His love is part of all of the paths he has led me one. His love is what binds them together and leads me forward on them. His love is what I have needed the most and what it has been so difficult to receive.

There is a lot of mush in my head Jesus so I am not sure what to say or even if I want to say anything. Sometimes I don't Jesus....Crying.

My little one I am here with my arms around you. I see everything that is on your heart my little one. I see everything that is worrying you and causing you pain. I know the things that you love and the things that you fear. I know your every desire my little one and all the empty places in your soul that need to be filled with our love my little one. I know everything about you and whether you say it or not I know what it is that you want to say my little one. It is not hidden from me.

It's hidden from me Jesus.....Crying.

My little one you are longing to know when the love that you need so desperately is coming. My little one I have promised you many things but love most of all. I know my dearest one that you have not understood what I am doing in this time or what it is that I am waiting for.

139

I don't want to talk about this. It just makes me cry.

But my little one do you remember the question in your heart that I said I was going to answer.

You said you were going to show me what love is. But I don't even know what you mean by that…..Crying

My little one whilst it is true that love has many facets and it is too big and wonderful to be fully discovered in this life it is possible my little one for you to know that you are fully loved, for the person that you are my little one and not for any other reason.

I don't want to talk about it.

My little one the wound that we have been healing is almost gone. There is very little to be seen of the wound that you had.

That makes no sense. It doesn't feel any better.

No my little one for the emptiness that was there still remains.

I don't understand what you have done and what you are doing or what you are going to do. I don't care. It doesn't make any difference if I understand or not…..Crying

Yes my little one it does. It makes some difference my little one for with understanding comes acceptance.

Acceptance of what?

Of our love my little one, a love that you have not been able to receive until now.

I don't believe….Crying

That is because you have not allowed yourself to understand my little one.

I don't want it. I'm tired of talking about it and I don't know what's the matter with me. Help me.

My little one do you think that you deserve our love?

No. Not even a little bit.

Why not my little one? You are my child, why should you not receive the love I have for you?

I don't know something like I'm not good enough. I'm nothing and nobody to anyone and you should go away and leave me alone. I thought I was better. Why do I still think those things?

Because we have gone deeper my little one. The lies that are in your heart go right to the core of you my little one and cannot be broken all at once. It takes time my little one and much healing and love.

But I don't see why I still believe it….Crying

My little one the things that hurt you formed the way that you think and the things that you believe about yourself. My dearest one do not be angry with yourself because all of your hurt is not yet gone. I am

healing you my little one. It will come.
Will it?
Yes my little one it will. My little one do you want to keep me out, do you want to keep daddy's love out of the emptiness you feel?
I think it's what I deserve. I can't have love. It's not for me.
Yes my little one it is. It is our gift to you. Will you accept our gift my little one now that you understand a little better?
I don't think I can have it….Crying.
But I say that you can my little one.
I don't know what to do.
Hold on to my hand my little one and allow me to lead you forward into daddy's love for you. He will not give you more than you can bear my little one. Little one my words are true. It is not wrong for you to receive our love for you. It is not wrong for the emptiness in your heart to be filled. It is not wrong for you to receive every good thing that we have for you. You are our child. We love you. Do not try to hide away my little one. You cannot hide from us.
I don't want to.
My little one this is a battle and you must choose just as you have done so many times before.
I choose you Jesus and you daddy but I need your help, because I am wanting to run away.
But my little one you are safe. You are safe my little one. There is nothing to fear from our love.
I know that in my head….Crying
Hold my hand my little one. Take one step at a time. If you need to stop we will stop. There is nothing to fear my little one.

I held on to Jesus hand. I was crying a lot because I was afraid. We started to walk along a narrow silver road. There was just enough room for me to walk alongside Jesus. It was more like a bridge really because there was a big drop on each side. All around it was cloud and rainbows like I have seen daddy before. Maybe that is as far as I have been before but now I was going further.

Why is the road silver?
It is the road to redemption my little one.
I thought we were going into daddy's love.
Yes my little one we are but we cannot get there without travelling along this road. It is a road that we must walk together my little one. You cannot walk it alone.
Why is there such a big drop Jesus?

Because my dearest one you must keep to this exact path. If you turn from it you will never reach daddy's heart of love for you.

What is this?

This is the entrance way my little one.

We came to what was kind of like an archway, I thought maybe it was shaped like a heart but I might have made that up. It looked like pink mist in there.

It is kind of warm and soft.

Yes my little one.

It is hard to describe but the pink stuff was warm and even though it looked like mist it felt soft like pillows. Like it was holding me and hugging me. It made me think of safe and warm. I think that I am too bad to be here. I don't think you want me here.

My little one, my dearest little one I have brought you here because this is where I want you to be. You are not too bad my little one. You are hidden in me. Our daddy sees my goodness when he looks at you. You are not too bad my little one. Shall we go a little deeper my little one?

Ok.

We walked through the pink stuff to where there were some sparkly silver curtains like a doorway.

This is a very strange place Jesus.

It is the place that you need it to be my little one. Daddy's love is being given to you in a way that you can accept.

I...ok.

So we went through the curtains. I didn't see it very clear because I just kind of crumpled up and cried and cried. I know that it was a room of comfort and it was full of soft cuddly toys. The whole room was soft and cuddly with pillows and comforting things.

It is too much Jesus…crying.

We can stay here for a little while my dearest one. One step at a time.

Ok. I want to see it.

It will become clearer to you my little one.

I just kept on crying. It was too much for me really and I wanted to run away but I stayed as long as I could.

My little one that is enough for today. Our journey into daddy's love will continue my little one but that is enough for now.

Being able to receive his love for us was so very difficult at first because it hurt so much. He told us that as his love went in the pain was washed out. That is why it was so very painful for us, which made it frightening and meant we could only receive a little at a time.

My little one our love for you is like an ocean in that it is deep and vast and wide, but we will only give it to you a drop at a time. We will not drown you little one, but we will teach you to swim and to immerse yourself in all that we are longing to give to you.

And you show me things and let me experience things but not too much.

No little one we are leading you gently by the hand. We know your heart little one we know that you are desiring so much more but we must go gently little one for there is still much healing to be done and a relationship to be built between us that will last little one and withstand all the storms of life.

Yes. You are making me strong in you.

Yes little one we are for revelation in itself will not make you strong, it is relationship which does that little one.

I keep thinking about something you have been saying in my heart for a long time. People talk a lot about your gifts Holy Spirit and how they want them.

Yes little one they do, though often it is for their own purposes little one.

That is bad Holy Spirit, but you have never talked to me about gifts you have been saying over and over that I will minister out of relationship and not out of gifts. What does that mean?

Little one I give many gifts to our children, gifts through which they are able to serve us and bless those that we send them to. My little one

there is something greater than this. Gifts are just that little one and they are good, but it is a greater thing to be filled with us, to be so full of us that you are overflowing with our love and our power little one. So that you are able to touch and affect the lives of others just because of who you are because of your deep and abiding relationship with us. That is far greater little one than any gift.

I think it would be better to be full of you than to have a gift Holy Spirit. I am not sure if I know how it is different.

Little one you can have a gift and it can be the greatest gift that has ever been given by us but little one the gift is not us, we give the gift but it is not us. To have a relationship with us that means that you are filled to overflowing with us, is to be able to give us to people little one, to be us to people. Little one people can have powerful gifts without being filled with us. They can minister in our power and cause many things to happen around them but that is not the same little one as being able to be us to people. There is no love in the gift little one, love comes from relationship with us.

Is that what Paul was talking about when he said that love was greater?

Yes little one. Gifts without love, gifts without us, are empty little one. You will minister out of your relationship with us. You will minister with love little one, you will show people who we are. You can only do this when you are rooted and established in us and in our love little one. You will not minister out of the gifts that are given to you, you will minister out of your relationship with us...which is far greater little one.

Jesus wanted me to receive his love in a way that not only healed me and set me free but built a relationship with him, the Holy Spirit and Daddy God so that he can flow through me to give his love away to others. Through everything he has done, all the ways he has led me, all the paths I have been on with him he has been making me strong in him, in the knowledge of his love for me.

I pray that out of his glorious riches he may strengthen you with power through his Spirit in your inner being so that Christ may dwell in your hearts through faith. And I pray that you, being rooted and established in Love, may have power, together with all the Lord's holy people, to grasp how wide and long and high

and deep is the love of Christ, and to know this
love that surpasses knowledge—
that you may be filled to the measure
of all the fullness of God.
Ephesians 3:16-19

Love has brought me healing and life. It has enabled me to stand in the truth of who I am and who Jesus is. But it isn't just for me, it is for me to give away to others so that they can know they are loved too, no matter how broken they are no matter how they feel or what they believe about themselves.

There is something that I have been noticing, but I don't really know what to do with it so I will just tell you what it is. I have been noticing that some Christian leaders say things that are not helping me. So these are the things I have heard, most of them from well known Christian leaders and some from my pastor. I have heard that Christians can't have demons, so I suppose that means if you do you aren't a Christian? I have heard that if you are insecure and don't think you are worth anything...then you are proud, that you are insulting God and that you are self-centered. I have heard it is impossible for people who don't love themselves to love others. I have heard that if you have been hurt by someone you should forgive them and let it go, like you can just do it all at once. I have heard that if you have MPD then you have a mental illness. I am wondering why it is helpful to say these things. I don't understand why anybody would say those things about people who are already hurting and feeling bad about themselves. I don't understand how people who love Jesus can say those things. If these things are true it makes me feel like I should go back in my hole and not ever come out again.

How will it ever be safe to come out if that is what people who love Jesus think? I don't want anyone to ever see me if that is what they are thinking. I don't think Jesus would say those things but maybe I am getting it wrong, because I get so many things wrong and they are all people who have known Jesus for a lot longer than me, so how can it be wrong what they are saying. Everything in this life is confusing.

My little one come. My dearest one just because people do not understand my heart for you, that does not mean that you have been deceived my little one. My love for you has not and will not ever

145

change. You are my beloved, my precious child and no matter how much you have been hurt, no matter how broken you are that will never change.

But why don't they understand Jesus?

My little one my people often misunderstand my heart, that is because they do not take the time to understand me, my little one. Sometimes it is too painful and too costly to truly understand my heart of love. My little one part of my calling on your life is to show people who I am, to show them my heart of compassion for those who are broken. My little one you will do this both in word and in deed. It will not be too much for you my little one for I will be with you.

I don't think people want to know about people like me Jesus. They think we are too much trouble and not worth bothering with.

But that is not my heart my little one, that has never been my heart. My dearest one your brokenness does not make you any less loveable to me, your brokenness does not make you less worthy of that love my little one. My dearest one I have come to bind up the broken hearted, not to leave you abandoned and alone, not to write you off and say you are too much trouble, not to condemn you or blame you because you have been hurt my little one. That is not my heart for you.

But I think we are too much trouble Jesus....Crying.

No my little one you are not. You are precious and you are loved. My little one there is not one of my children that is too much trouble for me.

But here in this world…

My little one I will give you everything that you need. I will give you people who will love you and care for you, for whom you will not be too much trouble my little one for they will see you for the blessing that you truly are.

Why do people say those things Jesus?

Because they do not understand my little one, they speak from the ignorance of their own hearts.

But if they have your heart inside of them Jesus, I don't understand.

My little one my people do not always understand what it is to be broken, nor do they want to understand my little one. It is easier for them to see the broken of this world as the problem of this world, but my little one the truth is that everyone is broken, those who cannot see it, are the most broken of all my little one. My little one all of humanity carries a brokenness within them, that is why I came my little one. Those who do not recognize their own brokenness and their need of me, are the most broken my little one for they do not recognize their need of me and so they never come to me to be healed and restored. Blessed are those who see their need of me my little one. You are so blessed.

But I still don't understand how..

My little one just because someone belongs to me and serves me, even those who serve me with all of their heart, that does not mean that they truly know me my little one.

That is hard for me to accept Jesus.

My little one I work through many people who neither know nor understand my heart for the broken. That is because I take their willingness my little one and I work through it. My little one this is not my desire for them. My first desire is that they should know me and love me with all of their hearts, that they should flow with my love first and foremost, but often they settle for less my little one, often they settle for power over love.

I don't understand people and I don't understand you Jesus. I don't understand.

My little one I take people where they are at and I work through them. It is not my desire that they should stay in that place my little one, I am always longing to take them forward, to lead them further into my heart of love for them and for others, but often they are content with what they have my little one. They do not want the pain of discovering their own brokenness, nor even the pain of seeing and truly understanding the brokenness of the people around them.

How can people who love you and serve you be so blind Jesus?

Because that is the human condition my little one. You have to be willing to see the truth...you have to seek it out.

I think the truth is a very hard thing to know Jesus.

Yes my little one in this world it is and so many are deceived even amongst my own people. My little one do not ever give up searching for the truth. Do not ever stop desiring it. The truth will protect you from many of the snares of the enemy my little one.

But, if even those people don't know the truth what chance do I have Jesus? I don't have any chance.

My little one all that you must do is draw closer to me, to follow me and let me draw you into my heart of love. I am truth my little one. When you know me you know the truth.

But..

My little one through you, through your life and all that I will make you to be, I will show the world the truth of who I am, and my heart for those who are hurting my little one. I will not leave this unchallenged. My dearest one it is always my heart that those who are in pain should be healed and those who are bound should be set free. That is my heart for you my little one and the way that I will do this is to love you. That is what my people most need to learn my little one, how to love as I do. I will help you my little one to show my people how to truly love.

I think that is too hard for me Jesus because I don't think I am very good at loving people.

My little one you understand more about my love, even now, than many of my children do. As you are healed and set free I will be able to flow through you unhindered my little one. You will show the world who I truly am and not who they have believed me to be, nor even who they would like me to be, for my love is not an easy thing to accept my little one. It challenges people to look beyond themselves to others my little one, it challenges them to see their own need and it challenges them to become more than they are, to surrender themselves into my hands of love and to trust and follow me with their whole lives. My little one there are many, even amongst my own people, who do not want to know the fullness of my love.

I don't know what to say Jesus because that is a terrible thing.

Yes my little one it is. My little one all that I have for you is to be found in my great love for you. Do not be troubled by what others may think of this my little one. You belong to me. Keep coming to me and I will give you all that you need, even if no one else ever recognized that need my little one still I am here for you.

Yes. Jesus, I don't know, how can you show people who you are through me?

Because my little one everything that you are and everything that you will have to give will have come from me. I am going to fill you my little one so that you will shine with my love. You will show them the truth of my love my little one, whether they are willing to accept it or not.

I want to be full of you Jesus. I am going to have to stop now because I am too tired. One day I would like to spend better time with you Jesus.

It will come my little one. Rest now and do not be anxious about what anyone else thinks. Remember my love for you my little one. Rest in the knowledge of my love.

Chapter 15

The Inside Path

One of the very first things Jesus spoke about was the path into his heart, that he was leading us into his heart of love for us. When Jennifer was just beginning to learn how to hear him, he gave us a vision of what he was doing, where he was leading us.

I saw a city which I understood to be old Jerusalem. There were many ways, through narrow alleys. The Lord was speaking to me as we moved down the streets.

I am taking you down narrow streets- some dark, some light. You must follow me closely or you will get lost. Follow me to the heart of the city where I dwell. That is where we are going. I am holding your hand. You need me to lead. You can't find the way. We will go in unexpected directions. There you will find my heart and we will dwell together. It doesn't matter how far it is because we are journeying together. It will be a sudden revelation- burst into revelation. Just hold on to me. We will get there.

I asked him can we run and he laughed a little.

Yes we can run.

We went down many narrow streets which were empty, deserted, taking many twists and turns. At the heart I saw a place of such beauty that I thought it was heaven. I asked him will I be dead when I get here. And he laughed and said no.

Right from the start Jesus began teaching us about reality, true reality. He began by leading us into the things of the spirit even before we knew about the bad things. We accepted the spiritual world as real through the dreams and visions he gave us. When we first learned about the bad things and about the alters, we had a lot of trouble knowing what was real and what wasn't, what was truth and what was lies. We didn't feel like we could trust anything. Not our own memories, what we thought we knew about our lives, about other people or even about ourselves. We couldn't even trust our own feelings because often they didn't seem connected to anything. We didn't know where the feelings and thoughts we were having came from. We were confused and unsure of everything and we didn't trust anyone. It was beyond frightening. But Jesus was there to help us discover what was real and true, beyond anything we could have discovered without him. We had to start from scratch because we couldn't take anything for granted. There was no certainty in anything.

I thought I'd write a quick response to your email. It's not always easy for me to organize my thoughts but I'll just give them to you as they occur. You ask why I would doubt that I was hearing God...why would I not? What is there that I can count as certain in my life, whether it's my inner or my outer life? I've never been the kind of person who felt they could be certain about anything. I always believe there's every possibility that I could be wrong. In the past year my whole life has turned out to be one big lie, my family, my past and even who I am. I have no real idea about the truth of any of these things. Why would I trust any of my thoughts, perceptions, feelings? How can I be certain of anything...I'm so afraid of believing lies that it's hard for me to believe anything and I certainly don't trust my own judgment. Then add to that the knowledge that I have so many different voices in my own head...who turn out to be other people and not me at all. HOW THE HELL AM I SUPPOSED TO BE SURE OF ANYTHING. You might think I'm sure the alters are real but I'm not...I sent you what 'they' said because I just don't know what else to do. I am so confused and distressed about all of that. When I got your reply to 'them' I just sat and sobbed for a very long time, because it really hit home that this is real and yet it seems so unreal. I don't want to be the responsible one. I can't do it anymore. If there are other alters there, I'm happy to hand it over. My only concern is for my children, as long as they are ok that's all that matters. Frankly, I think that one of the others could do a better job than me. I don't see I have anything to offer anyone, probably all my good qualities belong to someone else. This life has NOTHING that I want to hold on to. The idea of living in any kind of community, inner or outer, terrifies me. I feel completely trapped and unable to see any bearable options. What kind of future is there because I can't see anything...what is it I'm supposed to see? I'm so tired I don't even care anymore and all that there seems to be is a promise of is years of more of the same. I don't think I can do that. I don't want to do that. All I can seem to do at the moment is sit and cry or just be completely numb. I can't pray... apart from God please help me...that's the extent of my dialogue with him at the moment. I feel so lost and so trapped all at the same time. Sorry this is a pathetic ramble but that's how it is. I'm good at pretending most of the time, conceal and contain that's what I do in public. In private I unravel. There you are, the real me, whatever and whoever that is. I don't think anyone actually really knows me, they think they do but they don't really. Bye Jennifer.

We chose to trust Jesus and his reality because it was the only thing that made sense. It was the only thing that gave us any security. We knew that Jesus had led us to where we were, we knew because we could see it clearly. That at least seemed certain. We learned to trust what Jesus told us was real over and above anything we thought we knew. We had learned, in a really hard way, that what we thought was certain often wasn't. We had to open our hearts and minds to things, to realities and truths, that maybe we wouldn't have if all of our certainties hadn't been stripped away. Jesus became our only certainty. We clung to him. Without him I think we would have lost any sense of what was real and what wasn't. The certainty we needed went way beyond the truth of our own life. We needed to know what the truth of our past was, and of who we were, but it went beyond that to the bigger questions of truth and reality, to the truth of the unseen and the eternal, of the spiritual realms that we knew something of, but which didn't seem very real to us. Jesus showed us there is a greater reality than the one we thought we knew. Knowing that there were so many of us sharing one body made it necessary to believe in something more than what we knew to be possible. That was even more so when we learned about the inside world that the alters lived in. Either we were crazy, or it was true. There wasn't any other choice.

The more we trusted in the things of the spirit and accepted them as real, the more he was able to show us and teach us. He began with Jennifer of course, teaching her about dreams and visions and to hear his voice clearly. Then he began taking us to places in the spirit, like the attic where he took Jennifer and Aj. The Holy Spirit took Aj into the mountain of the Lord, where she had her own classroom and the Holy Spirit was her teacher. He taught her, and me of course, many truths that would help us on our journey, to help us understand about how to walk with him.

My little one everything that you do is done through me, everything that you experience is through me, everything that you hear and see is through me, that is my gift to you little one. I enable you to see and hear and perceive. I enable you to respond to us. I give you everything that you need to be the person that you are, living in our kingdom as a child of the King. It is through me that all of these things are possible my little one. That is why I say I am giving you a testimony. I am giving you a testimony about the King my little one.

I don't think I have really understood about these things Holy Spirit. Please keep showing me who you are.
Yes my little one. Do not be afraid because you do not yet understand. I am showing you many things my little one for I do not want you to be ignorant of these things. I want you to know and understand who I am in your life and all the things I make possible for you. This will give you confidence my little one and increase your capacity to grow and receive from us, from all of us my little one.
Because you are the spirit of the father and the son.
Yes little one that is so.
And you... it is because of you that I can hear Jesus.
Yes little one, I have given you that ability.
Thankyou Holy Spirit.
You are welcome my little one. I am longing to show you all the things that I enable you to do and to be, many of which you have not yet discovered.
I think you are changing something inside. I can feel it

happening.

Yes little one. I am changing your perception of what you thought you understood. I am bringing you truth little one.

Are you praying for me Holy Spirit?

Yes my little one I am constantly praying for you.

But that makes no sense to me Holy Spirit. Why would you pray to yourself?

I am not praying to myself my little one I am praying before the throne of the father from whom all things come.

So you have to ask the father?

Yes little one, as does Jesus...Because little one he is the source.

I am not understanding why he is the source and you aren't Holy Spirit?

Because that is how things are ordered little one. Even though we are all equal, even though we are all one, the father is the source, just as Jesus is the savior little one.

So like you have different jobs?

Yes little one a bit like that but not quite.

And the father is in charge of giving you things for us out of the storehouses of heaven maybe?

Yes little one something like that.

I know there is more Holy Spirit.

Yes little one there is much more.

So you go to the father and ask him for stuff and I suppose he always says yes to you because you are always agreeing. He wouldn't ever say no would he?

He would not ever say no little one, not to me and not to Jesus, for we know his heart completely, we are one with him little one.

So why can't you just go get the stuff yourself Holy Spirit?

Because the father is the source little one. I know you are not fully understanding but that is because there is still much for you to see and to learn.

Alright, so you and Jesus you both pray for me and the father gives you what you ask for because they are always good things.

Yes little one that is so.

But some things take time, though don't they?

Yes little one sometimes they take time to be made real in the physical sense but in heaven they are already real. There is no waiting in heaven.

153

So the father is not being slow to make up his mind or give you the stuff.

No little one. He is not slow to answer.

But the answer may be slow in getting to us?

Yes little one and there are many reasons for that which we will discuss at a different time.

I think that would be a big conversation Holy Spirit.

Yes little one it would.

So are you praying all the time Holy Spirit?

Yes little one I do not ever stop. I am constantly before the throne interceding on your behalf.

I expect you will stop when I am dead though Holy Spirit.

It changes little one but there are still things that must be asked for and received even in heaven.

Really?

Yes little one for the father will always be the source. It will not ever change little one.

Oh. I think heaven might be another day too or I will get confused.

Yes little one another day.

Why does it say about you groaning Holy Spirit?

Because when I am praying through you little one that is how it can sound and feel, for I am expressing things that you cannot understand and asking for things that you have no knowledge of. My prayers are deep little one, they go to the heart both of God and of man.

I don't know what to do with that at all Holy Spirit. Deep prayers, I get ashamed about my prayers. I think they are not very good.

Little one I will teach you how to pray effective, strong and deep prayers. That is part of all that I will give to you but little one do not underestimate the power of your prayers, you are heard and you are answered. Many words are not required little one. The true power of prayer lies in the heart.

But your words have power, don't they?

Yes little one they do but the words in themselves are not enough little one, it is the power behind the words that is important. This comes from the heart of the one who is praying little one.

I see, but I am thinking there is a way to release that power Holy Spirit is that right?

Yes little one it is and that is what I will teach you.

154

That is good Holy Spirit. I would like to pray prayers that make a difference.

Your prayers already make a difference my little one but there are different levels of prayers. I will help you to go deeper little one so that you can pray with greater power than you are able now.

When her turn came Blossum was taken on an inside journey with Jesus. That is when we began to see the inside path. Not that we hadn't always been on it of course, but Jesus showed us our path in a new way, to help us understand the journey we were on. He took Blossum on an inside path, that he told her was journey into his heart of love for her. It was a path that took her further into healing, into the truth of who we are and who he is. It was a path that led us forward into his purposes but most of all it was, and is, a path that leads deeper and deeper into his heart of love.

Blossum's path took us to the places we needed to go. It took us to Blossum Castle where we learned that our security is in Jesus, in his heart of love for us. It took us to the forest of strength where we learned that our strength comes from Jesus, and then on to the land of hope where we took hold of more of the hope that he has already put in our hearts.

As he led me forward, he took me on a path that led me through the forest of difficulty, through the land of rest, down the hill of change and finally down to the city of hope. It is this path that has given me the clearest picture of my journey with him. It is this path that has helped me see and understand the purpose and the direction I am moving in...it is this path that has taken me to the city of hope.

The inside path and the journey I have taken, have taught me about the reality of the spiritual world even when I was doubting what I was seeing. I have learned that everything I see and experience there has meaning. Everything is there to teach me or lead me, to encourage me or give me whatever I am needing. He took me into the forest of difficulty before I knew what was coming and how hard life was going to be for me. He used the inside journey to prepare me for what would come and to show me he had purpose in it. He used it to give

155

me hope and to endure through things I found overwhelming a lot of the time. It helped me to see the progress I had made, when I finally came out of the forest and my trust in Jesus grew because of all that the path had given me.

My little one your time in the forest has accomplished all that I desired. You have followed me faithfully. You have learned to trust and depend on me even when you could not see or understand the way that I was leading you, even when it seemed too difficult to continue you have held on my little one. You are so much stronger than you were but you are weary and now it is time for you to rest my little one.

I don't even know what you mean by that when I am working so hard and everything is so difficult. That isn't going to stop.

My little one you have been fighting many battles and breaking free of the things that have been holding you. That is what has made you tired my little one not the physical work that you have been doing though that is hard and tiring in itself. I know my dearest one that you are longing for things to change and they will but first you need to rest. You need to spend time with me. You need my instruction and my guidance. You need to see and to understand more clearly than you do now. This is a time when you can begin to see and understand my little one. Where I can fill you and heal you and give you my strength for the journey that is ahead of you. I know my dearest one that you are so very tired and that is why you need to stay just for a little while my dearest one. You need to receive what I have for you. You need to prepare for the time that is coming. You need to know and understand more clearly than you do now what I will ask of you in the months that are ahead.

My path has led me to the city of hope, that was its destination. The city of hope is a place in the spirit, a place in the heart of Jesus that he has made just for me. A place where I can receive all that he has for me, where I can learn and grow and be who I am made to be. I am hidden in his heart at all times, but I am never standing still. He is always drawing me deeper. My path has brought me to the city but my journey into his heart continues. There is much more to discover, more love to receive, more to know and to do...and become. My path, though different, continues on into the city he has given me.

What is a city my little one?

A place where people live. A kind of community I suppose.

It is a place of life my little one, a place where people are connected to each other. They live together, work together, play together.

Yes. Ok.

And what is at the center my little one?

I don't know. It depends on the city, oh, the heart of the city.

Yes my little one and do you know what the heart of your city is?

I suppose it is you Jesus. It is your city. I know you gave it to me but it is still yours.

Yes my little one it is. The heart of the city is love and life and joy and hope and everything that I am my little one. The center of the city is what makes the city what it is. Without it the city would lose much of its life and identity.

Yes I see that. I am not understanding your point though Jesus.

My little one the city that is ahead of you is made up of many different kinds of people, all of them are in need of me my little one. But it is not just a city of people, it is a city of people who are connected in love to me. A city which will bring light and hope to other cities my little one.

So my city has connections to other cities?

Yes my little one it does.

I suppose daddy has a city.

Yes my little one, all of my children do.

And our cities are connected and all of them center on you.

Yes my little one that is so.

Ok, but I think I am missing the point.

My little one when you think of the city what do you see?

Walls, buildings.

But not people my little one. Not me.

That's because what I can see from here is walls and buildings Jesus. I've never been in the city. I've never seen the people.

But you have seen me my little one.

Yes....

My dearest one you are always walking towards me. Even though I am taking you to a new place the journey remains the same. The destination is the same. All the time you are walking towards me my little one. The difference is that along the way there will be many people for you to reach. There will be those who are lining the streets, coming out to meet you. There will be those who are hidden away.

There will be those who want to walk away from you my little one, and some who will try to attack you but your journey and your focus is the same. You are walking towards me. I am at the center my little one. I am at the center of you and I am at the center of the city I have given to you.

It is all about you.

Yes my little one. It is not about you nor is about the city as such it is about me my little one. Everything is centered upon who I am. You are walking towards me carrying my light giving it away to those who need it the most. You walk with me and for me my little one. You are hidden in me. There is nothing that you do and nothing that you are that is separate from me.

That makes me feel safe Jesus.

Yes my little one.

And like it isn't a heavy burden to carry because it is about you and not about me.

Yes my little one.

Hmm. I don't know if that changes anything Jesus. Maybe it changes everything. I am not sure.

I want you to look at the city again my little one.

The walls are glowing white Jesus. I suppose that is you and your protection over the city.

Yes my little one it is. What else do you see?

I see the stream is flowing into the center of the city.

Yes my little one it is.

That is your presence and your life.

Yes my little one I am in the city.

Are there different levels Jesus? I know I am looking at walls, but maybe there are different levels.

Yes my little one there are.

And I suppose, no I don't know. What do the levels mean?

The deeper you go into the city my little one the greater your influence. The deeper you go the more life you will bring.

Ok, but why are there levels?

It is to do with my power and my presence my little one. As you draw close to the heart of the city you are also growing closer to me. The closer to me that you are the more I can flow through you to others.

Ok, so to begin with I will be at the first level. I suppose there is a journey to do even when I get to the city. Is that what you are showing me?

Yes my little one there is.
Ok but really Jesus. There is enough to think about on this part of the journey.
I know my little one but it does not hurt to look ahead.
Maybe once in a while Jesus. I know I need to remember it is all about you and not about me.
Yes my little one you do.

Seeing as Jesus sees opens up new possibilities. It gives me hope when there seems no reason to hope. It tells me who I am and who he has made me to be. I see the world as he sees it only as he helps me to, I can't do anything on my own. My path has taught me that. I need him to live this life, any life. I need him to see the purpose in it and to fulfill that purpose. A purpose he has planted in my heart from the very beginning. A purpose the enemy has tried so hard to destroy but has only succeeded in making it possible. Like when they tried to destroy Jesus and his purpose by killing him, having him die on the cross. All they did was make it possible for him to fulfill his purpose which was to bring us life through his death.

Help me see Jesus. Help me see like you do.
Do you want to my little one? You will see many things that you do not want to see.
Will I? What will I see Jesus?
True reality my little one, a reality that will break your heart for my children.
Like yours is broken.
Yes my little one.
Do you want me to see Jesus? I mean am I ready to see?
You need to be strong enough my little one so that what you see does not overwhelm you but only causes you to hold on to me tighter and to trust me with those you love and those that I love also.
I was thinking more of seeing this Jesus, the pool and the spiritual world, but I suppose it all goes together.
Yes my little one it does. Seeing cannot be separated my little one. Seeing the spiritual realities of the world around you and within you is a blessing my little one but it will also bring you pain as you see the true nature of the darkness that my people are living in and the hold that the enemy has on them. It will help you my little one to help them

but it will not be easy for you.

You are making me wonder if I want to see Jesus. It is hard enough now when I only see a bit. I suppose, I don't know. As long as I know that it's not something I have to fix but that I need to trust you with it all, I don't know Jesus. How can I know? This world is already overwhelming to me a lot of the time.

I know my little one but remember it is not only the darkness you will see. You will also see the things of the kingdom my little one, the things that I am doing. More of who I am in this world and in my children.

And that will be wonderful.

Yes my little one it will.

Is it something you want to give to me Jesus?

Yes my little one it is as you are ready to receive it.

Seeing and understanding.

Yes my little one.

Seeing true reality like you do.

In part my little one. I will not enable you to see everything.

Because it would be too much for me.

It would not help you my little one.

Why?

Because my dearest one it is only as some things remain hidden that you are drawn to me for the answers you need.

Well...I know seeing and understanding for me won't mean knowing and understanding everything like you do Jesus.

No my little one it won't.

I suppose some things would be too much.

Yes my little one they would. I will enable you to see and understand my little one but only as much as will help you.

Well if it is a gift from you I know it is good Jesus. And if I need it then, I do. And if you want me to have it then I say yes to it.

That is good my little one that is very good.

Jesus understands about suffering, about sacrifice and how hard it is to follow the path that makes it possible to fulfill our purpose. He understands that it is hard and painful and the battles that face us every day. He is with us on our path. He made the path for us, each of us according to our own need and our own purpose. He is there to help us, to guide us and

160

protect us. To pick us up when we fall and to teach us and heal us and most of all to love us and show us the truth, as we walk with him. We can't walk the path without him. We aren't meant to...because it's all about relationship with him. It is a path meant for a purpose, to help us become who we are, not on our own but with him, so that we are free to live the way he meant us to live, being who he made us to be in a world that will often tell us we aren't ok.

Not that I have already obtained all this,
Or have already arrived at my goal, but
I press on to take hold of that for which
Christ Jesus took hold of me. Brothers
and sisters, I do not consider myself yet
to have taken hold of it. But one thing I do:
Forgetting what is behind and straining
toward what is ahead, I press on toward
the goal to win the prize for which God
has called me heavenward in Christ Jesus.

Philippians 3:12-14 NIV

www.ingramcontent.com/pod-product-compliance
Lightning Source LLC
Chambersburg PA
CBHW040332070426
42446CB00051B/3464